Aldous Huxley
A Beginner's Guide

ONEWORLD BEGINNER'S GUIDES combine an original, inventive, and engaging approach with expert analysis on subjects ranging from art and history to religion and politics, and everything in between. Innovative and affordable, books in the series are perfect for anyone curious about the way the world works and the big ideas of our time.

Aldous Huxley
A Beginner's Guide

Kieron O'Hara

ONEWORLD

A Oneworld Paperback Original

Published by Oneworld Publications 2012

ISBN 978-1-85168-923-1
eBook ISBN 978-1-78074-080-5

Typeset by Cenveo Publisher Services, Bangalore, India
Cover design by vaguelymemorable.com
Printed and bound in Great Britain by
TJ International, Cornwall, Padstow, UK

Oneworld Publications
185 Banbury Road
Oxford OX2 7AR
England

Stay up to date with the latest books,
special offers, and exclusive content from
Oneworld with our monthly newsletter

Sign up on our website
www.oneworld-publications.com

Contents

Contents

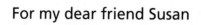

For my dear friend Susan

Preface

Aldous Huxley's celebrity has not dimmed in the half-century or so since his death. Dozens of his works remain in print, some with introductions by authors as eminent as Margaret Atwood and J.G. Ballard. Googling his name produces as many hits as Iris Murdoch, Doris Lessing, Graham Greene, Evelyn Waugh and Jeffrey Eugenides put together. His most famous novel, *Brave New World*, regularly appears in lists of the 'best books' (for example, as the best work by an English author in a *Le Monde* poll at the end of the century), and at the time of writing it enjoys a ranking comfortably in the top 500 bestsellers on amazon.com, amazon.co.uk and amazon.fr (it is 618th on amazon.de). We can see Huxley's likeness at the National Portrait Gallery, and on the cover of The Beatles' album *Sgt Pepper's Lonely Hearts Club Band*; the rock band The Doors took their name from one of his books. He is simultaneously part of high culture and popular culture.

Yet these bald statistics and facts raise the question of why we continue to read Huxley, and the deeper one of whether we should. He wrote in a world very different to ours, where democracy was threatened first by fascism, then by communism, where the power of science was becoming visible, where the mass media and mass production were emerging, and where traditions, canons and value-systems were being reassessed after traumatic decades of violence and bloodshed. He wrote as an old order was being swept aside by a morally ambiguous progress. In many ways, Huxley's world is barely recognisable from a twenty-first-century standpoint. Our world is the *result* of the revolutions Huxley describes.

The nature of the revolutionary forces themselves, Huxley's subject matter, is irrelevant; they have done their work, they cannot be reversed. Huxley lived in a world of possibilities which from our perspective are simply yesterday's speculations. What can he possibly have to say to us?

To understand that, we have first to understand what Huxley was saying to his contemporaries. The aim of this book is to enable a reader to approach the work of Aldous Huxley understanding its context, both in terms of Huxley's own thought, and the politically and intellectually fraught times upon which he commentated. In the five decades of Huxley's writing career, he changed his position on many substantive issues. So the world changed too, although a common thread of violence and totalitarianism runs through the middle of the twentieth century. His first stories appeared while the Battle of the Somme raged; his final work appeared just a year after the Cuban Missile Crisis. To be able to read Huxley, one needs to know what stage his thought had reached when he was writing, particularly as he often worked out his ideas laboriously in print over a series of books or essays. As Joyce Cary argued, Huxley's 'revolt was moral. It was founded in hatred of the lie.'[1] But what Huxley would put in place of the lie depended on the state of his thinking, and the social, technological and political context of his writing.

To that end, this book describes Huxley's life in seven stages, six of which cover his writing career. This is an artifice, like any such division, but it produces the best clustering of his large output. Each major chapter contains three sections. The first sketches the main events in his life – important for understanding Huxley, who incorporated many autobiographical and semi-autobiographical elements into his fiction.

The next 'Works', gives a short summary and background of each of Huxley's prose works. I have not included the poetry, of which there were half a dozen collections of original work between 1916 and 1931, partly because his *oeuvre* is slight, and partly because there is rarely a *philosophical* insight in his poetry that is not better expressed in prose; I have also left out his several plays and adaptations for similar reasons. I have included all the novels, the original collections of short stories and essays, the full-length political and philosophical works, the travel books, the biographical histories, the anthologies and four pamphlets and Forewords, that were published in Huxley's lifetime and therefore approved by the author himself. Altogether that is forty-one works, each of which has a short section devoted to it in the appropriate chapter.

The third section, 'Thought', attempts a synthetic summation of Huxley's thinking in each particular period. Certain themes, such as language, value, education, popular culture, ideology and sex, recur, but always with a different twist, depending on Huxley's development at the time.

This book is therefore intended to orient the reader to Huxley's work, to allow him or her to follow Huxley's thought on a particular topic, or to understand a particular work by Huxley in the context in which it was written. It is not a substitute for deep critical analysis. I have referenced useful sources and quotations, but have not given page references for quotations from Huxley himself. This is partly to avoid the book being taken up by dozens of footnotes, but mainly because most of Huxley's works appear in several editions, and so page references are unlikely to be helpful. This Beginner's Guide is not aimed at the scholar with access to all of Huxley's first editions. I hope the reader will be motivated to dig deeper.

My final prefatory task is to thank Oneworld for editorial support and wise words on how to present Huxley's work, and an anonymous reader of the text who gave me several useful comments, and who filled a few glaring gaps in the 'Further reading' section at the end. Of course, the responsibility for the completed text is entirely mine.

1

'Inescapable social destiny', 1894–1920

The Huxleys and the Arnolds

Aldous Huxley's intellectual and social inheritance was extraordinary. His grandfather was one of the greatest Victorian scientists, Thomas Henry (T.H.) Huxley (1825–95), known as 'Darwin's bulldog' for his tireless popularisation of secular evolutionary theory. The 1860 Oxford debate pitting T.H. against Bishop Samuel Wilberforce (a well-known high churchman known as 'Soapy Sam') was one of the great set pieces of Victorian public life; famously, when asked by Wilberforce whether it was through his grandfather or his grandmother that he claimed descent from an ape, Huxley replied that although he would not be ashamed to have a monkey for an ancestor, he would be ashamed to be connected with a man who used his great gifts to obscure the truth. He was sceptical about religion, and coined the word 'agnostic' to describe himself. Yet he did not fight shy of ethical dilemmas, arguing that although mental characteristics are a product of evolution, values are culturally determined, and hence one is not absolved from the duty to make ethical decisions simply because certain aspects of one's mind are biologically determined.

His role in public debate made him a household name, but he was also a pioneering zoologist and anatomist in his own right. He also was an important educationalist, promoting scientific education at secondary level (in the London School Board), tertiary level (with the Royal School of Mines, now a constituent college of Imperial College, London) and for adults (he was Principal of the South London Working Men's College). The combination of respect for science, concern with the public welfare, and interest not only in ethical issues themselves but also in the way they are influenced by scientific understanding and technological development, was imbued in the Huxley family.

Aldous's other grandfather was literary scholar Tom Arnold (1823–1900), which linked him with the dynasty of another Victorian patriarch (his great-grandfather) Thomas Arnold, legendary headmaster of Rugby School, immortalised in the novel *Tom Brown's Schooldays*. Tom Arnold's older brother, Huxley's great-uncle, was the poet, social critic and philosopher Matthew Arnold (1822–88). One of Tom's daughters was Mary Augusta Ward (1851–1920), who as Mrs Humphry Ward achieved fame as a prolific and bestselling novelist, of which her best-known effort was *Robert Elsmere*; the other, Julia, in her own right intelligent enough to earn a first-class degree in English from Somerville College, Oxford, married T.H. Huxley's second son Leonard. A photograph shows her engaging and keen, looking intensely at the camera, with haunting effect.

The family inheritance was concentrated remarkably in Leonard's children – extraordinarily, Aldous was only the third most successful of the brothers, in worldly terms at least. Julian (1887–1975) became an evolutionary biologist and humanist philosopher very much in the mould of T.H. (there is a famous photograph of him sitting on his grandfather's knee), although he was also a prominent promoter of the now-discredited 'science' of eugenics. This caused him some problems with both Catholics and communists when he became the first Director-General of the United Nations Educational, Scientific and Cultural Organization (UNESCO) in 1946, and his six-year term was cut to two. He was a great populariser – in the 1930s he ran London Zoo, controversially increasing access for children – and became a well-known radio celebrity, appearing in programmes like *The Brains Trust*.

He was knighted in 1958. Yet even Julian pales next to his half-brother Sir Andrew Huxley (b.1917), winner of the 1963 Nobel Prize for Physiology and Medicine, member of the Order of Merit, Master of Trinity and President of the Royal Society (as was T.H.). Yet although Aldous thought fondly of his half-brother, they do not seem to have been particularly close (Sir Andrew has written that Aldous and Julian 'were more like uncles than brothers'[1]).

The Victorian Age saw the gradual decline of aristocracy, and of the sway of religion over the English – the theme of Matthew Arnold's stunning poem 'Dover Beach'. The loss of certainty brought about by Victorian ideas, including Darwinism and the Industrial Revolution, left a vacuum in the centre of public life. Arnold's brilliant *Culture and Anarchy* diagnosed the problem and prescribed a solution in terms of the protection of culture as the best that has been thought and said. Gradually, the landed gentry were replaced in public life by a group of meritocratic families whose nobility was self-consciously grounded in intellectual achievement and public-spirited responsibility. The Huxleys and the Arnolds were joined by the Wedgwoods/Darwins, the Macaulays, the Trevelyans and others who believed that their intelligence, knowledge and social standing gave them responsibilities for improving the lot of humankind in practical ways. These public values were formative for Aldous. His inheritance was a rich one, but it came with a lot of baggage.

Three tragedies, early successes and a family

Aldous Leonard Huxley was born on 26 July 1894, in lovely English countryside near Godalming in the county of Surrey, the third son of Leonard (b.1860) and Julia (b.1862). Julian was the eldest of their children, followed by Noel Trevenen (b.1891), always known as Trev, then Aldous, and finally his sister

Margaret (b.1899). The sprawling extended family was close; Aldous in particular was close in age, temperament and feeling to his cousin Gervas (b.1894), while other cousins such as Laurence (b.1890) and Joan Collier were frequent and welcome visitors.

Huxley's early childhood appears to have been idyllic and appreciated. The brothers were firm friends. Aldous adored his mother, who appears to have had a shining integrity, deep human sympathy and great authority. His father, an assistant master at Charterhouse, seems to have been a pleasant, limited man who communicated with the children at more or less their own level, fond of puns and japes, but nevertheless – or, given the rarefied environment, consequently – not really respected by the boys. Huxley's later writings are full of thinly disguised memories of endless summer days, sunshine, explorations and expeditions. He enjoyed collecting moths, playing conkers, rambles, picnics and, on their frequent holidays in Switzerland, climbing hills.

He was well-loved, bright and unusual, but not immediately academically distinguished. He was tall with a large head, which, when he was very young, he sometimes could not hold up, earning him the affectionate, if insensitive, nickname of 'Ogie', short for 'Ogre'. He spent long hours contemplating, in Julian's words, the strangeness of things.

In 1902, his mother realised an ambition of opening a girls' school, Prior's Field, near their home, initially with seven pupils – five day girls, one boarder (who brought her dog) and Aldous. The school, still going today, was an immediate success, even if its curriculum was tailored to Mrs Huxley's strengths (literature was a priority, with day trips to Shakespeare matinées – but a number of girls failed their Lower Certificates in mathematics). After that, at the age of nine, Aldous went to a prep school near Godalming where he was stoical in the face of bullying and bad food. He enjoyed acting – his Antonio in *The Merchant of Venice* was apparently a show-stopper – and published his first poem, about sea horses, in the school magazine.

His upbringing could not have been better or happier. In 1908 he went to Eton, with his best friend Lewis Gielgud, the brother of Sir John, and was happily getting to know the place when the first of three devastating blows fell. His mother had been unwell, and in September, unbeknown to Aldous, cancer was diagnosed. Before the end of November she was dead. Huxley only discovered the horror when he was brought to see her for the last time; she was in pain, frustrated and angry at the cosmic injustice. The loss to the family – and the school – was profound. Worse, the happy family home was broken up. Julian was at Oxford, Trev and Margaret went to stay with Mrs Humphry Ward, joined on holidays by Aldous, and Leonard moved to Bayswater, where he lived alone.

Huxley's time at Eton was well spent; he enjoyed learning, had a quirky wit and did not waste his time on schoolboyish matters. He spent most of his time reading, yet was not unsporty; already over six feet four, he was bored by cricket but enjoyed the high jump. But in 1911 his academic career was halted abruptly; no one was initially worried by his swollen, red eyes, but he was soon almost completely blind, just about able to distinguish night from day. *Keratitis punctata* was diagnosed, a violent inflammation of the cornea, and in the days before penicillin and antibiotics there was little to be done.

Completing his education at Eton was now out of the question; his precious collection of now useless books was sent to his father's house. Aldous himself stayed sometimes with Mrs Ward, and sometimes with Gervas's father, his uncle Dr Henry Huxley. Gradually the condition subsided, but the inflammation had badly damaged the cornea. With extraordinary stoicism he adapted to his new situation, learning to read and write in Braille. The problem with Braille, he complained, was that one could not skip while reading tedious authors such as Macaulay – one had to read every single word; the advantage, as he told Gervas, was that one could read in bed at night without getting one's hands cold.

He also taught himself various piano pieces, painstakingly learning the right hand part, then the left hand part, and only then, having committed them to memory, playing the whole piece. Once a partial recovery had been made, he insisted on bicycling himself to the station, despite not being able to see where he was going (he would follow Gervas's mother). Most extraordinary of all, he wrote, on a typewriter, a novel of 80,000 words – substantially longer than this volume – which he never saw, and which is now lost. He never recovered more than partial sight; one eye was capable of perceiving light, while the other could make out shapes. He could read with the aid of a magnifying glass and drops of an atropine solution in his better eye that would keep the pupil dilated, enabling him to see around an opaque patch in his cornea.

In 1912 his father remarried, to a much younger woman called Rosalind Bruce (she was actually younger than Julian and Trev). The Huxley children were not close to their father and although Rosalind seems to have been generous and welcoming to them, they did not reciprocate. Aldous instead began to travel, and to try to regain his independence, first journeying alone in Germany, and then wintering with his uncle John Collier in Montana, where he somehow learned to ski. In 1913, he was able to begin to get ready for his Oxford Matriculation; he went to stay with his brother Trev, already ensconced as an undergraduate approaching his finals.

Trev was well-liked, extremely kind and unselfish, though sensitive and nervy. Nerviness was a Huxley trait: T.H. had been prone to depression, and Julian, now beginning an academic career in the US, suffered a nervous breakdown in 1913 which caused him to break with his fiancée of the time. Yet Trev felt things more keenly than even they. He and the rest of the family were deeply disappointed when he only got a second-class degree. Aldous began at Oxford in October 1913, while Trev sat for the civil service exam – once more underperforming.

By the summer of 1914, Trev had descended into depression, partly owing to poor results, partly through the weight of unfulfilled familial expectation, partly through overwork and over-exercise, and partly through worry over Julian's breakdown. Little is known of the events of that summer, but he seems to have begun a relationship with a young housemaid. The strict social stratification of the time would have made such a relationship problematic, to say the least, for its participants; Trev suffered his own breakdown, and was confined to the same nursing home that had sheltered Julian the previous year. One Saturday, though he appeared cheerful, he never returned after a walk, and over a week later his body was found hanging from a tree.

Aldous's grief was deep; it pours out in letters he wrote at this time. In many of his later novels he worked through his feelings; many incidents allude to the three tragedies, characters are based on Julia and Trev, and the metaphors of light, darkness and blindness recur over and over again. Oxford provided him with few distractions; by the time he began his second year, he was virtually alone. Britain was at war, and his able-bodied friends had joined up. As hostilities commenced, Huxley's views as expressed in his letters were conventionally pro-war and anti-Boche, and he made several attempts to enlist, yet of course he never made it past a medical examination.

That is not to say that he struck an unimpressive figure. Extremely tall, he was very much the dandy and even something of a ladies' man. The future novelist L.P. Hartley, who briefly had rooms on the same staircase at Balliol before being called up, recalled that:

> I had never known anyone like Aldous. His voice, his rangy height, his elegant clothes, his noble white brow, crowned with a patch of unruly black hair, his mysterious rather glaucous eyes … peering through the oblong magnifying glass he used when he was reading – these left an ineffable impression. Culture had found a mortal envelope worthy of itself.[2]

Huxley did well at Oxford, entering prizes (winning only some of them), hating Anglo-Saxon and introducing himself to the finest French literature, including the first volumes of Proust's epic *Remembrance of Things Past*, all the while reading laboriously with his glass, and typing verse and short stories with a little portable on his knees. His fascination with mysticism began here, as he investigated William Blake and the German Lutheran Jacob Boehme from an impeccably twentieth-century sceptical standpoint. He was en route to a distinguished intellectual career, taking a first-class degree in English in 1916.

Yet the turning point in Huxley's early career came not via the university, but instead as a result of a social call, when a friend took him for a day out to Garsington Manor, near Oxford. The new owners Philip and Lady Ottoline Morrell curated a menagerie of interesting people, and it was thought, correctly, that the grandson of T.H. Huxley would be a fine addition. Philip was a Liberal MP, one of the few statesmen who had opposed the war with Germany (this would cost him his seat in 1918), but was comfortably off, having vast inherited wealth from the Morrell brewing interests familiar in and around Oxford.

Lady Ottoline (*née* Cavendish-Bentinck, from a highly aristocratic family) was a different kettle of fish altogether. Her marriage with Philip was open, and their joint interests in liberal politics, as well as liberality in both hospitality and sexuality, meant their coterie, containing the cream of Bloomsbury, was perhaps the most talented assembly since the great Parisian salons of the Enlightenment. Lady Ottoline's lovers included Bertrand Russell, Augustus John and Roger Fry, while at Garsington one might expect to see Herbert Asquith, John Maynard Keynes, Clive Bell, Vanessa Bell, Virginia Woolf, D.H. Lawrence, Lytton Strachey, Katherine Mansfield, John Middleton Murry, Mark Gertler, Siegfried Sassoon, Dorothy Brett, Dora Carrington and T.S. Eliot. Lady Ottoline was 'arty beyond the dreams of avarice' in Huxley's words, affected, shy and religious, romantic, kind and eccentric. She and Philip kept up their generosity even when they had run through their money, but their kindnesses were often repaid by mockery, gossip and backbiting (not least in some unkind fictionalisations by Aldous, but with greater maliciousness by Mansfield, Strachey, Carrington and Clive Bell).

Having graduated, Huxley was unsure what to do; as he wrote to Julian, the solution of the heiress had its attractions. That winter of 1915, Huxley was introduced to Lawrence and his larger-than-life German wife Frieda, and the latter's silvery tongue persuaded the reserved Aldous to sign up for one of the former's schemes to set up a colony of like-minded free-thinkers in Florida. Fortunately for all concerned, it fell through. Of the real-istic solutions to his problem, he was torn between, and equally unenthusiastic about, journalism and teaching. Teaching in the end it was, with a term at Repton; he hated it. Meanwhile his poems and stories were beginning to appear, and by 1916 he had published enough to bring out his first volume of poetry, *The Burning Wheel*, a well-received collection with the characteristically Huxleian theme of hope confounded.

He continued to visit Garsington, and was by now thoroughly indoctrinated with the anti-war views de rigueur in that house. In lieu of war service, he volunteered for work on the land – mainly chopping trees at Garsington – alongside a number of conscientious objectors in the Morrells' sphere, such as Russell and Clive Bell. By a fortuitous set of coincidences, a young, pen-niless, rather gauche Belgian refugee, Maria Nys, came to stay. She was somewhat overwhelmed by the aristocratic sophistica-tion and competitive intellectual fireworks. Indeed, she was very unhappy early in her stay, at one point attempting suicide. But Aldous wooed her patiently, finally proposing on the lawn at Garsington in the summer of 1916.

The engagement was hard; they had no money, and were often apart. They wrote to each other every day. Maria left Garsington and moved to London, but could barely support herself.

Aldous moved in with his father (who by now had left teaching to become editor of the *Cornhill Magazine*) in Hampstead. Eventually, Maria had to rejoin her mother and sisters sheltering from the war in Italy.

After an awful year, he got a post at Eton in autumn 1917 while his poetry was gaining an audience. His second small collection, *Jonah*, was published that year, followed by *The Defeat of Youth* in 1918, and during the school holidays he managed to get away and rejoin his rarefied social circle. The war finally ended in November, allowing Maria and her family to return to their father in Belgium, but even so Aldous did not have enough money to join her. Finally, in 1919 Middleton Murry offered him a job on the editorial staff of his literary journal *The Athenaeum*, and things were suddenly set fair. His father lent him money, he was able to resign from his teaching job, and he finally travelled to Belgium to see his fiancée for the first time in over two years. He found his prospective in-laws somewhat provincial, but they got on. Sadly, there was to be no inherited fortune. The Nys family, previously comfortably off, had been financially wiped out by the war.

Aldous and Maria married quietly in Belgium in July 1919, shortly before his twenty-fifth birthday; she was approaching twenty-one. She was small, especially compared to her giant of a husband, gamine, somewhat insecure; she was no intellectual, but had a practical streak (she not only tolerated, but even helped plan, his later *amours*,[3] and occasionally indulged herself with lovers as well). They settled down in a tiny flat in Hampstead, which Aldous decorated himself, and lived a life of genteel poverty, speaking French by choice together, English with friends. They had a daily maid but no cook, and managed for themselves with few frills – not even a sink or a cooker. Work was tolerable; Huxley wrote around two hundred reviews for *The Athenaeum*, as well as more articles elsewhere, and the poems kept coming too. He signed a contract for a book on Balzac, which, sadly, was never written.

Family matters dominated early 1920. His beloved Aunt Mary, Mrs Humphry Ward, died in March, while after a difficult pregnancy for Maria, their son Matthew was born on 19 April. Aldous's fourth, and perhaps best, collection of poetry, *Leda*, appeared in May. But in literary terms the most significant event had already occurred in January, with his first book of prose – six short stories and a little play, collectively entitled *Limbo*.

2
Ironist, 1920–5

Life

Life for Aldous and Maria was pleasant, but wretchedly poor, in Hampstead. Their poverty was not the grinding sort that wrecks lives – they could go over to Garsington for the weekend easily enough, and they could still afford a nursemaid – but the work was hard, and at one point Huxley was holding down three jobs. As well as *The Athenaeum*, he worked in a book club, and as a theatre critic for the *Westminster Gazette*, which drove him to distraction as he spent virtually every night and most afternoons watching plays and writing about them to tight deadlines. The combination of seeing how bad most plays were instilled in him the belief, never rescinded, that he could and should write a successful play himself.

His celebrity was ready to take off; he had already charmed many of the significant cultural figures of the day by sheer personality. Dame Edith Sitwell, poet and lifelong friend who rivalled Huxley for notoriety as a representative of the post-Great War avant-garde, described him thus:

> Aldous Huxley was extremely tall, had full lips and a rather ripe, full but not at all loud voice. His hair was of the brown, living colour of the earth on garden beds. As a young man, though he was always friendly, his silences seemed to stretch for miles, extinguishing life, when they occurred, as a snuffer extinguishes a candle. On the other hand, he was (when uninterrupted) one of the most accomplished talkers I have ever known, and his monologues on every conceivable subject were astonishing

floriated variations of an amazing brilliance, and, occasionally, of a most deliberate absurdity.[1]

Nevertheless, hard work was still needed. Not only was he skilled in developing intriguing lines of thought on life, art and politics, but he was also getting the knack of churning out decent prose to deadline, and of engaging with a mass audience, rather than his small, refined, highly educated and aristocratic social set. Advancement came, and he was able first to drop the book club job (the club had gone bankrupt anyway), and then to move from *The Athenaeum* to the Condé Nast organisation, where he helped launch *House & Garden*. He had to keep the *Gazette* job, but was pleased to move on from theatre to music criticism.

The little place in Hampstead was so small that the baby could not help but disturb his father as he wrote, so the Huxleys took the drastic step of separating: while Aldous wrote and saved, Maria and Matthew went to stay with her parents in Belgium. They were apart, minus a snatched meeting in Paris, for five months, before some Italian friends of Maria found them a cheap place in Florence, where they moved in April 1921.

Huxley, who had only briefly visited the North of Italy before, was enchanted. He was able to take a long rest, and mixed with the English diaspora, including the Sitwells and William Walton. Batteries recharged, the Huxleys moved to the Tuscan seaside town of Forte dei Marmi, where Aldous wrote his first novel, *Crome Yellow*, in two months. This was the beginning of a long love affair with Italy, its people and its art. In-between periods of hard writing, they enjoyed their leisure time with visits to Pisa, Siena, Lucca and Rome, where Huxley was enchanted by the sixteenth- and seventeenth-century sculpture and architecture. When he returned to England in October, he was already scheming to work out whether he could earn enough by writing to live cheaply in Italy.

Crome Yellow appeared in November. It was a brilliant satirical debut which worked on several levels. It was an ironic farce (the irony was much less savage than the early works of Evelyn Waugh in the next decade, yet without Huxley's pioneering work Waugh might have struggled to avoid alienating his audience). It played with ideas. It had broad comedic moments. It was also a *roman-à-clef*, with recognisable and none-too-flattering caricatures of Garsington, Lady Ottoline and Philip Morrell, Bertrand Russell, Dorothy Brett and others (including Aldous himself); some took offence, and there was a long estrangement from the Morrells. Huxley's family hated its unkindness and cynicism. In vain Huxley pleaded that the novel's characters were mere marionettes with superficial similarities to their originals, and that his apparent cynicism was a result of his facing up boldly to the arbitrary and often unsatisfactory nature of reality, where – to quote the title of one of his early stories – there was rarely a 'happily ever after'.

Outside the immediate Huxley circle the novel was a roaring success, both critically and in terms of sales. The Huxleys moved into a flat in Paddington, which they shared with Matthew's nursemaid Bella, and Aldous commenced work with Condé Nast. Maria's younger sister Suzanne lived with them for several months in a somewhat odd but apparently innocent *ménage*, sharing a room with Aldous and going with him to the concerts he was reviewing for the *Gazette*, while Maria stayed in during the evenings and slept alone; Matthew and Bella had a room together. The atmosphere was remarkably harmonious given the sleeping arrangements, and Huxley was able to continue his literary work alongside his journalism. In May 1922 his second book of stories, *Mortal Coils*, was published.

Summer was once again to be spent in Forte, while Bella went to what is now Poland to visit her family, taking Matthew with her; Maria went to Italy initially leaving Aldous and Suzanne together. Aldous followed a few weeks afterwards. They saw more of Italy and toured Central Europe, taking in Salzburg and Vienna. Return in the autumn saw Maria and Aldous in a new place in Kensington, and 1923 brought a deal with Chatto & Windus that gave Huxley some financial independence; over the next three years, he was to supply them with two books of fiction a year, one of which should be a novel, in return for an advance payment of £500 per year.

All might have gone smoothly, but the Huxleys' unusual domestic arrangements, perhaps unsurprisingly, went alongside an element of sexual freedom and exploration; Maria tolerated Aldous's affairs, while she was also not averse to some variety, apparently with women as well as men. There are disputes about the evidence, but Nicholas Murray has argued that Maria's suicide attempt at Garsington was connected with a strong passion she had conceived for Lady Ottoline. A long affair that Aldous conducted with Clive Bell's long-term lover Mary Hutchinson was initially seen on *Mary's* part as a means of getting close to Maria in order to begin an affair with *her*.[2]

Despite their sophistication, in 1923 Aldous fell head over heels in love with Nancy Cunard, avant-garde poet, political activist and heiress to the Cunard shipping fortune (although she refused to touch her allowance). She impressed everyone; Sybille Bedford, who knew her, assembles a set of representative quotes about her.[3] 'Impeccably outrageously extravagantly courageous, generous, violent, self-destructive, fanatically wrong-headed, waywardly elegant, incarnately alluring'; 'a fiery and furious angel'; 'a terrible messenger descending with a fiery sword upon bourgeois hypocrisy'; 'made of alabaster and gold and scarlet, with a face like Donatello's Saint George'; 'tigress-dragonfly'; 'Nancy's voice was a miracle. And so was the way she walked … she flowed swiftly forward … like a cheetah.' Cecil Beaton's portrait of her taken in 1930 bears out these breathless epithets.

Although Aldous's infatuation was briefly consummated, Nancy was not interested. Nevertheless, he followed her around, absolutely in thrall, for months, on one occasion leaving Maria in Florence to go back to London to see Nancy. He fell behind with his writing commitments. In the end, Maria lost patience and insisted they went back to Tuscany, where he immortalised Nancy, writing her out of his system, in his second novel *Antic Hay*.

After the Cunard entanglement, life got back to what passed for normal. The Huxleys bought their first car, a Citroën. Maria learned to drive, enjoyed driving, while Aldous loved the rigmarole and paraphernalia of cars and became interested in Grand Prix racing; she indulged him by driving very fast (his defective eyesight meant of course that he could never take the wheel). Their journeys were later replayed in his collection of travel essays *Along the Road* and his third novel *Those Barren Leaves*. They mingled with the English, including the well-known novelist and essayist Norman Douglas, and tolerated the buffoonish Italian fascists, at least until their house was brusquely invaded and searched on a flimsy pretext in 1925.

Antic Hay was another success, outselling *Crome Yellow* but once more offending his family; the description of the lead character's mother's death, echoing that of Huxley's own mother Julia in detail, was thought highly distasteful by Leonard. Aldous followed up with more expertly crafted stories ready for a collection, *Little Mexican*, which appeared in 1924. Meanwhile, the contracted book on Balzac was quietly forgotten; no advance had been paid, so the publisher, Constable, agreed, reluctantly, to cancel the project. *Those Barren Leaves* was written in the summer of 1924, and *Along the Road* in the autumn. *Those Barren Leaves* outsold the first two novels; although it was larger in scope and in some respects more ambitious, Aldous quickly came to the conclusion that it was an inferior work.

At the end of June 1925, after their bad experience with the *fascisti*, they seemed to find themselves at a crossroads, plans at best vague, wondering what was farther afield (they had toured Tunisia earlier in the year). The Huxleys found a drastic solution; they parked Matthew with his grandmother in Belgium, moved to London, wound up their affairs (including submitting the story collection *Two or Three Graces*), and set sail for Suez, aiming to travel around the world.

Works

Limbo (1920)

Huxley took the seven pieces (all but one previously unpublished) that made up *Limbo* to Chatto & Windus in late 1919. They were the first company he approached, and they immediately accepted the offering and became Huxley's British publishers throughout his career. Influenced by his readings of the French symbolists (nineteenth-century poets who rejected realism, such as Baudelaire, Mallarmé and Verlaine), and in particular the early prose of André Gide, the pieces are varied, all fantastic in a mild, whimsical, British way, laced with the powerful irony that would be characteristic of all Huxley's work.

There is a wide formal variation – one novella, one long story and a play, as well as four short pieces of traditional form. In 'The Death of Lully', a Spanish libertine is witness to the death of the (historically real) mystic Raymond Lully, and hears his last testimony, though we do not discover whether or how he will profit from the encounter. In 'The Bookshop', Huxley muses on humanity's 'wearisome condition' for the first time, rationalising the moving effect of hearing Berlioz's arias sung by an elderly bookseller.

The longer pieces justify their length. 'The Farcical History of Richard Greenow' tells the strange story of a young man who discovers a new personality within himself, a female writer who earns him fame and fortune. The story plays around with the compromises between art and hack work, against the background of a fictionalised version of Garsington, renamed 'Crome'. In the bitter parable 'Happily Ever After' a young man, another self-caricature, wanting to put his mind in order prior to being called up to the war, manages to alienate his uncritically patriotic family, and fails to consummate his affection with his guardian's repressed daughter. After he is killed at the front, she gives herself to his badly maimed friend.

Crome Yellow (1921)

As a model for his first novel, Huxley took the nineteenth-century writer Thomas Love Peacock's satires on the intellectual mores of romanticism – such as *Headlong Hall*, *Nightmare Abbey* or *Gryll Grange* – wherein several lightly disguised caricatures of leading figures of the day would talk, sometimes brilliantly, sometimes ludicrously, about the matters of the day in an artificial, closed environment; the ideas were the real characters. Everyone conversed, but no one succeeded in communicating.

This was a perfect model for Huxley who scandalised his immediate circle by casting them in various parts in his novel. *Crome Yellow* describes a week at a house party at Crome, a lightly disguised version of Garsington and its guests, including Dorothy Brett (Jenny, a deaf girl who sees people more clearly than they see themselves), Dora Carrington (Mary, a determinedly 'modern' bluestocking and advocate of free love), Bertrand Russell (Scogan, a talkative sceptic who knows everything and is convinced by nothing), and the artist Mark Gertler (the Byronic Gombauld). The hosts, Henry and Priscilla Wimbush, were immediately identified as the horrified Philip and Ottoline Morrell; Henry is a nice, bumbling historian, while Priscilla is a silly woman desperate to have extra-sensory perception.

Huxley also put himself in the novel, in the form of the naive and ineffectual Denis Stone, whose arrival and departure form the arbitrary start and end points. He falls in love with Anne, the Wimbushes' niece, is persuaded that she is indifferent to him, plans an elaborate leave-taking (he fakes an urgent call back to town by sending himself a telegram), and discovers that his love was requited after all; too late, he has to leave. Throughout his stay at Crome he has been unable to act effectively. Everything he does, including his attempts to write, go wrong (Huxley enjoyed himself composing Denis's not-so-good poems).

Along the way, stories and parenthetic diversions are interpolated, some of which anticipate later ideas in Huxley's *oeuvre*. Henry tells the tale of tiny Sir Hercules of Crome, who attempted unsuccessfully to build his own Lilliput; the fantastic grotesquerie reminds one in atmosphere of the later novel *After Many a Summer*. Another ludicrous and entertaining digression is Sir Ferdinand's Elizabethan treatise on household plumbing, *Certain Privy Counsels*. One of Scogan's lengthy discourses predicts the automation of childbirth and its effects, prefiguring *Brave New World*. Vast state incubators would supply the world with the people it needs for its industry, while dissociating love from propagation. Denis is appalled; Anne thinks 'it sounds lovely'.

Mortal Coils (1922)

Huxley's next book contained stories (and a short play from 1920) written while his journalistic career was burgeoning. The title was the first of his literary quotations, a metaphor for life from Hamlet's soliloquy. Pluralising the term neatly implied the distinct nature of different types of existence and points of view. The stories are of high quality, and one of them, the modish murder mystery 'The Giaconda Smile', Huxley would revisit and rewrite both for the stage and for the movies. In that, a selfish man with an invalid wife simultaneously carries on an affair with a vulgar girl, and a flirtation with a spinster of his own class. When his wife dies, he marries the girl against his inclinations, prompting the spinster to take a terrible revenge. 'The Tillotson Banquet' narrates the rediscovery of an elderly artist, now frail and senile, eclipsed by his art – a sort of reverse Dorian Gray.

In other stories Huxley began his literary exploration of the Italy he had come to love. In 'Green Tunnels', a tale of multiple ironies, a girl completely misinterprets a message in the sand, while in 'Nuns at Luncheon' a lady writer painstakingly pieces together the strange career and doomed love life of a nun who finds sex, temptation, shame and mortification.

On the Margin (1923)

On the Margin collected a series of essays largely written for *The Athenaeum* under the pseudonym 'Autolycus' (the 'snapper-up of unconsidered trifles' from Shakespeare's *The Winter's Tale*). Huxley was a natural essayist, and much of his fiction – particularly *Crome Yellow* – is peppered with discursive comments on life, politics, science and art; his essays on many topics stand up to scrutiny today, and he usually expresses the cutting edge of opinion of the day pithily, straightforwardly and provocatively.

On the Margin developed his vein of superior mockery of the idiocies, unrealistic aspirations and inadequacies of urban life in the 1920s. In 'Pleasure' he makes his first attack on mass entertainment and the passivity it engenders, removing the habit of thought and creating dependence on the offerings of movie moguls and sensationalist publishers; he gives his account a political twist by arguing that degenerate, passive minds are unlikely to administer democratic institutions in a vigilant and engaged manner. In 'Accidie', he describes how those who demand stimulation (whether sex, drink, high society or drugs) need ever-stronger doses, in the inevitable scarcity of which they sink into a state of slothful boredom which was a mortal sin in medieval times but a badge of honour for the decadent young things of the day – a theme he was to explore in several novels. In 'On Re-Reading *Candide*', he undercuts this thought by arguing that Voltaire's famous sceptical conclusion that to do the right thing one should cultivate one's own garden is somewhat less compelling today when the gardens (i.e. lives) of the bank clerk and the shop-girl are so uninteresting.

On the Margin was never conceived as a whole, and the cumulative effect of the essays is to make the reader feel that the only possibilities are a boring suburban existence or a meaningless metropolitan one. There seems to be no way forward; Huxley's eloquent and insightful (and undeniably snobbish) critique of the immediate post-war ennui allows no relief or optimism.

Antic Hay (1923)

Huxley's second novel appeared to great applause. It tries to extend the Peacockian form of *Crome Yellow* in the less constrained environment of London's high society, inevitably opening out the action and allowing much greater engagement with and development of the characters. The title is a quotation from Marlowe's *Edward II*: 'My men, like satyrs grazing on the lawn, shall with their goat feet dance an antic hay', alluding to the absurd and meaningless goings-on, and the merciless way in which they are described.

Huxley represents himself as another clever passive creature, Theodore Gumbril, like Huxley a master at a public school, who decides to make his fortune (unlike Huxley) by patenting a splendidly ridiculous yet borderline plausible invention; as he sits on a hard seat listening to an interminable sermon from the headmaster of the school at which he teaches, he suddenly gets the idea for Gumbril's Patent Small-Clothes, a pair of trousers with a pneumatic seat which can be blown up to cushion the wearer's posterior. Liberated, Gumbril tries to cut a swathe through the world by adopting the more extrovert persona of a Rabelaisian man, complete with false beard. Other real people appeared in the novel disguised, not least Nancy Cunard as bored temptress Myra Viveash, able to control men but finding it ultimately unsatisfying – a misogynistically drawn character-type that would recur several times in Huxley's *oeuvre*.

Every character is deceived and self-deceived. Some characters wrongly believe they love, or are loved; others, equally deluded in the opposite direction, believe they can enjoy physical passion without romantic attachment. Shearwater, a great scientist, only understands his statistics and research while his wife sports with most of the other male characters. Lypiatt the painter has the shallow world in perspective, but cannot transcend it; his paintings are no better than Cinzano advertisements. The self-consciously satanic Coleman enjoys provoking self-disgust in his friends and lovers. Irony abounds as characters' self-images are juxtaposed with the views of outsiders. The memory of the Great War cannot be shaken off.

The book is funny and dark, and its negativism almost unre-deemed. The one moment of genuine contact, a brief liaison between Gumbril and Emily, is besmirched when Gumbril mocks the tender episode to entertain Mrs Viveash and Coleman. Gumbril's sad remembrance of his mother's death undermines the message of God's love in the windy sermon of the Reverend Pelvey, M.A. Leonard Huxley disliked the book on account of this retelling of his wife Julia's death, but Gumbril's father pro-vides a positive note with his utopian vision of a rebuilt London based on Christopher Wren's plans after the Great Fire of 1666. Even that vision has to be sacrificed for the compromises of grubby reality, as Gumbril Senior is forced into selling his pains-takingly built model.

Little Mexican (1924)

The better stories in *Little Mexican* were written in Italy over the winter of 1923/4, and once again the collection was centred around a farcical novella, 'Uncle Spencer', one of the few works in which Huxley directly addressed the Great War, exploiting his experiences with the Nys family in Belgium. A man remembers his childhood visits to his Uncle Spencer who has bizarrely inherited a sugar beet mill in Longres, a fictionalised version of St Trond. On one such visit, a strange troupe of 'Tibetan Devil Dancers' plays at the bawdy annual fair, and one of the dancers, a Tamil cobbler whose name can only be rendered as Monsieur Alphonse, is courted by the pious sister of Uncle Spencer's house-keeper, and settles down to his trade.

The narrator is in Longres when war breaks out, and he vainly tries to persuade Uncle Spencer to leave. He and M. Alphonse are interned together with a plethora of other odd people, including Emmy Wendle, a cockney male impersonator, with whom he falls in love. Alphonse pines to death in captivity, but not before making a series of predictions all of which, bar one, come true. The one exception is that Uncle Spencer will marry Emmy; the story ends with the narrator and his uncle searching theatres, agencies and lodgings across London to find Emmy, by now effectively a creature of his own construction.

Little Mexican is more uneven in tone and quality than earlier collections. The best of the group is 'Young Archimedes', about an unschooled Italian peasant child, Guido, who shows appreciation for the finest music. His talent is fostered by more or less selfishly concerned adults, but he grows out of music, preferring the equally abstract and beautiful world of geometry. Forced into a music college in Florence, poor Guido pines for his books of Euclid, and in despair throws himself from a window.

Those Barren Leaves (1925)

Huxley's third novel is a further development of his technique. The claustrophobia on which the Peacockian form depends is diminished; the plot is more intrusive; characters develop organic-ally; it is formally more ambitious, using both first- and third-person narration. There is some tentative authorial musing about how the characters' dilemmas could be resolved. *Those Barren Leaves* is much less nihilistic in tone than *Antic Hay*. The title alludes to the importance of leaving behind the old ways of thinking, via Wordsworth's 'The Tables Turned', from the *Lyrical Ballads* (a key moment in the development of English Romanticism), which argues that the wisdom of nature exceeds, and is more valuable than, human wisdom:

> Enough of science and of art;
> Close up those barren leaves;
> Come forth, and bring with you a heart
> That watches and receives.

Huxley had been pondering an Italian novel since discovering the glories of Tuscany. The hostess, Mrs Aldwinkle (another send-up of poor Ottoline Morrell), assembles a cast of English eccentrics at her *palazzo*, imagining that she is perpetuating a long tradition of erudite gatherings of poets, philosophers and artists. Her *salon*, however, is definitely second rate – Francis Chelifer (another of Huxley's self-deprecating self-portraits) is the editor of the *Rabbit Fancier's Gazette*; Mr Falx is a political hack; Lord Hovenden is an upper-class twit interested only in fast cars; Mary Thriplow is an unsuccessful novelist; Cardan, a wordy sceptic not unlike Scogan from *Crome Yellow*, is an ageing hedonist only too conscious of his mortality, and so reduced in the world that he is in effect a professional guest. When he woos Grace Elver, a 'half-wit' (Huxley's words) with lots of money, he is shocked into the realisation that his philosophy is hopeless when she dies suddenly and painfully after greedily imbibing rotten fish.

Huxley's major fiction had until now gleefully and industriously pointed out the culs-de-sac and contradictions of self-consciously modern thought, but *Those Barren Leaves* makes a first attempt at resolution via the character of the cynical womaniser Calamy, who at first unenthusiastically seduces Mary. Impressed, like Huxley himself, with the variety of experience and diversity of sources of truth, he seeks solitude in order to meditate on what ultimate reality might be. At the end of the novel, he tries, and fails, to persuade Chelifer and Cardan that illness, decay and death can be transcended by the pursuit of a mystical unity. As he is left alone once more, the glory of his surroundings, particularly a limestone crag 'glowing with its own inward fire' reassures him that he is on the right track.

Along the Road (1925)

Following a year or so of manic motoring around Italy, *Along the Road* was written between October 1924 and January 1925 (published in September). Its winning combination of travel pieces and artistic criticism develops Huxley's theory of the importance of different, incompatible, yet equally legitimate points of view. He was always fascinated by science, but he did not privilege it; it competed with the different perspectives offered by art, morals, and even the opinions of the ignorant. Travel allowed access to other ways of looking at the world; things that were 'given' as common sense in one society might seem madness in another. Huxley favours the encyclopaedic artist who crams in detail, Balzac or Breughel, and in one essay describes his favourite reading matter during travel as a volume of the *Encyclopaedia Britannica*. The travel pieces illustrate his enjoyment of Italy in particular, and his appreciation for the geometric forms of Renaissance Rome (the essay 'Rimini and Alberti' recalls Gumbril Senior's laments for the lost ideal of Wren in London), the paintings of Piero della Francesca and even the flat landscape of Holland – all described in strikingly visual fashion, despite the author's severe handicap.

   Along the Road is not restricted to musings on travel and art, however. Huxley's characteristic social concern and futurology constantly feature. He describes popular music and low culture, and wonders how the rapid improvements in technology will affect the balance between work and leisure. His essay on Holland debunks many of the assumptions of the Enlightenment that human nature will inevitably progress; he prefers instead to explore the parallels between those living today and the cavemen of Altamira.

Two or Three Graces (1926)

As will be seen in the next chapter, Huxley was strongly influenced at the end of the 1920s by D.H. Lawrence. Ironically, in the long title story of *Two or Three Graces*, a Lawrence-like character, Kingham, fascinates and charms music critic Dick Wilkes in just the same way as Lawrence fascinated Huxley (who, let us not forget, was the music critic of the *Westminster Gazette*). Extraordinarily, however, this was a coincidental case of life imitating art. Kingham is not Lawrence, whom Huxley had only met once at the time of writing the story.

Wilkes meets a married woman, Grace Peddley, whose temperament and character change, chameleon-like, with her companion. With her husband she is homely and loving, while with Wilkes she becomes entranced with music. Wilkes introduces her to a showy, shallow artist, with whom she starts an affair, adopting his bohemian ways, although she remains the stereotypical housewife with her bourgeois husband. Jilted by the artist, she falls into a relationship with the charming but controlling irrationalist Kingham, who takes her on an emotional odyssey from which suicide seems the only escape.

The other stories in the collection are also concerned with the humiliations associated with class. In 'Half Holiday', a depressed clerk thinks he can ingratiate himself with a couple of aristocratic girls, but they reward his gallantry with money, not friendship. In 'Fairy Godmother', an orphaned girl's guardian tries to exert control over her sister, while in 'The Monocle', a nouveau riche young man uses the eponymous optical instrument as a prop to make himself feel secure in company – unsuccessfully.

Two or Three Graces was the last of Huxley's works to appear during his earliest phase, the stories written in 1925 but published in 1926 just before he returned from his round the world trip. It is ironic indeed that Kingham is made to say that a sensitive man can't go round the world and come back with the same philosophy of life as the one he started with. This turned out to be true of Huxley, though, writing prior to his voyage, he cannot have known it would apply to him. Maybe he was already hoping that a more positive outlook would emerge from his experiences. As it was, after this work he left satirical criticism behind, and began his attempts to find meaning and gain sympathetic understanding.

Thought

Huxley's early comedies are at their best extremely funny, and often coruscating about the emptiness and hypocrisy of post-war society. Yet, as has often been remarked, the dissection is somewhat emotionless, a scientist running experiments on his creatures. There is evidence that Huxley came to think that comedy and satire were essentially limited forms; three decades later he wrote in *The Devils of Loudun* that 'in pure comedy there is no identification between creator and literary creature, between spectator and spectacle. The author looks, judges and records, from the outside; and from the outside his audience observes what he has recorded, judges as he has judged and, if the comedy is good enough, laughs.' Huxley's readers certainly laughed, but were firmly locked outside the characters' worlds.

Huxley was keen to explore the nature of society and reality. Why do we do what we do? What drives our social machinations? Literature, philosophy and religion provide reasons for our actions – but are these not merely post hoc rationalisations of more basic drives? Are we not simply machines, driven by sex, or money, or recognition? Are we not restricted and defined by our social milieu?

The 'wearisome condition'

What impressed Huxley most were the psychological contradictions in people – hypocrisy, weakness of the will, self-deception. He concluded that we exist upon several levels, and we should not expect consistency between them all. He was impressed with an early statement of the problem in *Mustapha*, a verse drama of 1609 by Fulke Greville, Chancellor of the Exchequer under James I, first Baron Brooke, one-time owner of Warwick Castle, poet, playwright and soldier. Most of Greville's work is now neglected, but the 'Chorus Sacerdotum' is often anthologised.

> Oh wearisome condition of Humanity!
> Born under one law, to another bound,
> Vainly begot and yet forbidden vanity,
> Created sick, commanded to be sound:
> What meaneth Nature by these diverse laws?
> Passion and reason self-division cause.
> Is it the mask or majesty of Power
> To make offences that it may forgive?

Like many Elizabethan and Jacobean poets, Greville saw literature as an activity situated within, and commenting on, a wider context – a special, but not privileged, way of looking at the world. Literature could not survive merely by reference to its own history, traditions and tropes; the result would be nonsense that would fail to connect with lived, perceived reality. Huxley very much agreed that the multiple realities Greville described, the 'wearisome condition', was the only proper subject matter of literature.

He first quoted Greville in 'The Bookshop', and continued to use this idea as a reference point throughout his career. Virtually all Huxley's works comment on the wearisome condition of humanity to some degree, and more often than not it acts as the source of comedy or satire.

The crisis of value

The implications of Greville's insight that people are 'born under one law, to another bound' are massive. Huxley mercilessly ridiculed the value-systems of the day that vainly attempted to describe the world from a consistent point of view, arguing that they granted human actions and ideas a dignity he did not believe they warranted. Religion was humbug – not because it was false, but because it invited hypocrisy. Patriotism, nationalism and communism were secular religions for those with too little willpower to resist the oratory of their leaders. Convention was honoured more in the breach than in the observance, while private moral rules tended to be very adaptable indeed when applied to oneself, even when the basis of very scathing moral judgements about others. Romance was no more than a roundabout route to sex, and romantic ideas could never stand comparison with the reality of sex, betrayal, bodily fluids, illness, obesity, imperfection, pomposity and boring conversation with which lovers have to cope. In Huxley's fictional world empty rule-sets and value-systems were either ignored or outdated, and those most vocal about defending them transgressed them most enthusiastically.

Science could uncover hitherto unsuspected facts about the world, and describe it with accuracy and reliability, yet its apparent certainty led the unwary into two terrible errors. First, the undeniable increase in knowledge led to an unjustified faith in progress. Greater knowledge implied that one could plan more successfully, and that one could bypass or repair the misfortunes of life – but equally with the same knowledge one could build ever more terrible weapons, or ever more pointless gadgets to titillate jaded appetites. Second, as science grew in scope, and explained more and more things, it created its own ideology (usually known as positivism, following the nineteenth-century philosopher Auguste Comte) that science was the *only* source of knowledge, explanation and value. Yet there were many sources of information, and the human condition was all about negotiating between difference and diversity; as Denis remarks upon seeing Jenny's caricatures of him in *Crome Yellow*, 'we are all parallel straight lines' that will never meet. This was one of Huxley's earliest philosophical realisations; his first collection of poetry, *The Burning Wheel*, contained 'Two Realities', in which two people see a horse and cart go by. The first gazes in wonderment at the cart's beauty, while the second is disgusted by the horse's droppings. Same reality, different and equally legitimate human responses.

Huxley was adamant that the increase in scientific knowledge, though a good thing in its own right, would not necessarily make us better people, make society more rational and humane, or compensate for our loss of confidence in other sources of value. The character of a childlike scientist, unconcerned with anything unconnected with his work, disconnected from the society around him, recurs throughout Huxley's career. He appeared for the first time as Shearwater in *Antic Hay*, blissfully ignorant of his wife's cuckolding, who falls comically in love with Mrs Viveash and tries to remove the bothersome infatuation by insanely pedalling on an exercise bicycle.

This early nihilistic philosophy hit a nerve (Evelyn Waugh wrote that Huxley was 'then so near the essentials of the human condition'[4]). Huxley's appearance on the literary scene coincided with the end of the First World War. Modernism, a wide-ranging movement mainly concerned with constructing new systems that made little or no reverential reference to tradition, which promiscuously spawned experiments in art and philosophy from futurism to surrealism, Bauhaus to Leninism, the twelve-tone system to jazz, was the inevitable result of the catastrophic collapse of the sustaining assumptions of civilisation. Huxley, who was as knowledgeable about the old as he was well-versed in current trends, and who (once the horror of the war had become clear to him) had no sentimental attachment to the old ways, was perfectly placed as commentator and guide.

Sex and romance

In his novels, Huxley's characters were social beings in search of meaning. But on top of that, they were animals as T.H. Huxley had argued sixty years earlier, and therefore they were also after sex and status. Their clever talk was just another version of the swindle, the chat-up line, the con, the showing-off.

Away from his typewriter, Huxley seemed to enjoy sex, and got his fair share of it, but he rarely communicated pleasure in his books. For Huxley the novelist, romantic love was one more false, tackily sentimental value, while sex was a demeaning animal act. His lovers have to put up with being cuckolded, terrible diseases, sadistic cruelty, dying children, a lack of communication, guilt, regret, and even in one bizarre case being dive-bombed by a dead dog.

Sex is something men and women seek; it never gives happiness or leads to closure. It produces either failure, or guilt, or betrayal. Romance is similarly misleading; the ideal ignores the realities of life, the decrepitude of bodies and their unwillingness to perform, the pressure, as the critic Cyril Connolly famously put it, of the pram in the hall. The narrative of perfection undermines the attempt to live one's life alongside another human being. Only Dante got it right, Huxley sometimes suggests, living with a flesh-and-blood wife while platonically adoring an unattainable vision from the past.

Did anyone get sex right? D.H. Lawrence, perhaps. As early as 1924, when the two had met but were not yet firm friends,

Huxley was writing in an essay entitled 'Fashions in Love'[5] that sex should be 'cheerful and spontaneously animal'. Huxley as a rule did not care for the animal side of humanity, but in this case he was reacting against what he saw as a tendency, characteristic of the age, to over-analyse. 'We are becoming rather too self-conscious about our instincts' thanks to Freud and Marie Stopes. Still, even that was better than Puritanism or Victorian prudery. Not until *Point Counter Point* towards the end of the decade did a happily and successfully married couple appear in a Huxley novel.

The general outline of Huxley's attitude to sex is already clear from *Limbo*, in particular 'Happily Ever After'. His characters were drawn with quite a limited palette from which he rarely diverged throughout his career. A number of types crop up over and over again, created in this early period but continuing as templates for later novels. For example, he would often portray himself in a lightly disguised fashion as an intellectual with a highly developed mentality but emotionally very cold and even dead, unable to show love, intellectually responding to others but unable to empathise (Denis in *Crome Yellow*, Gumbril in *Antic Hay*, Philip Quarles in *Point Counter Point*, Anthony Beavis in *Eyeless in Gaza*, Jeremy Pordage in *After Many a Summer*). These Huxley-substitutes would be joined by cynics (Coleman in *Antic Hay*, Spandrell in *Point Counter Point*, Mark Staithes in *Eyeless in Gaza*), predatory figures in the manner of the mythological Circe (Mrs Viveash in *Antic Hay*, Lucy Tantamount in *Point Counter Point*, Mrs Thwale in *Time Must Have a Stop*), wise if prolix old men who would place the sexual hi-jinks in philosophical perspective (Scogan in *Crome Yellow*, Cardan in *Those Barren Leaves*), and a few other recurring types.

His male characters are rarely capable of satisfactory performance, are timid, romanticise women unrealistically, and are either hamstrung with guilt because of some past misdemeanour, or shocked when the object of their desires turns out to have sexual feelings too. His women are either promiscuous, pretentious, sadistic, cloyingly sentimental or simply absurd. Gumbril's Proustian realisation that 'most lovers … are in love with somebody else – their own invention' was echoed by Calamy and exemplified by Uncle Spencer. The upshot is that love is either a projection of one's own desires and fantasies onto an unfortunate and inadequate other, or humiliating loveless debauchery. Each is bound to lead to disappointment. The battle line was drawn in *Limbo* and *Crome Yellow*, and trenches were dug in *Antic Hay*. After that it rarely moved.

Layers of meaning and early flirtation with mysticism

In Huxley's early books, there was no meaning to be had, and the brilliance of the wits of Crome and elsewhere was merely a modern version of more antique humbug. Many critics and readers from the 1920s have testified as to the intoxicating effect Huxley had upon them. Huxley rubbed one's nose in it; he destroyed the pretentions of the older generation that had plunged Europe into a stupid and frighteningly destructive war (it is worth recalling that most of Huxley's readers at this time would have been recently bereaved), but he denied that the fashionable wits and thinkers of the Jazz Age made much sense either.

Huxley's usual narrative stance is down-to-earth but not commonsensical. He enjoys using the terms of science to ridicule pretensions to love, art, contentment or happiness. The same incident is often described using emotional language at first, and then the passionless language of science; deep drives are made to seem like random causal effects of electrical charges in the brain, or secretions in the stomach. The logical positivists, who believed that all knowledge came from experience, and could only be accurately expressed via the language of science, provided the philosophical backing for Huxley's method at this time. He must have been aware, at least in outline, of the logical positivist creed; the reductionism of Moritz Schlick, Rudolf Carnap and the Vienna Circle took a good deal of inspiration from Huxley's friend Bertrand Russell's *Principia Mathematica* (written with A.N. Whitehead), while Wittgenstein's *Tractatus Logico-Philoso- phicus*, another key text, had been championed by Russell in Britain.

In this resolutely modern world, one would expect that the mystical world 'beyond the veil' would be scorned as meaningless, and indeed the pretensions of characters such as Mrs Aldwinkle and Mr Barbecue-Smith, author of *Pipe-Lines to the Infinite* (from *Crome Yellow*) are roundly satirised. Yet for all that, Huxley seems to have had an abiding interest in mysticism. He retained his interest in the works of Jacob Boehme (he reviewed Boehme's *Six Theosophic Points* anonymously in *The Athenaeum* in 1919), while there is a strong streak of secular mysticism – in the sense of a revelation of aspects of the self through direct experience of insight brought by memory – in Proust, whom Huxley admired from his first reading of *Swann's Way*. His first collection, *Limbo*, contained a serious portrayal of a mystic ('The Death of Lully'), and a suggestion of the transformative power of mystical philoso- phy, while in *Those Barren Leaves* mysticism is explicitly mooted as a solution to the crisis of value. Calamy's conversion is uncon- vincing, but for all Huxley's cynicism and scepticism his attraction to mysticism was beginning to surface in his rational thought.

Why should Huxley sublimate his mystical streak? This would not be the only time that his professed adherence to a particular outlook, and the demand for consistency, would lead him to deny things to which he would otherwise have assented. His scepticism and ironical stance would naturally lead him to reject mystical ideas as being contentless, yet there is nothing self- contradictory about the wearisome condition of being bound by several different and apparently incompatible laws. Indeed a scep- tic should welcome such epistemological chaos, preventing any particular view about humanity gaining precedence over the others. Why should mysticism be singled out for satirical treatment? Could the problem be its universalising tendency, the oft-made claim of mystics to have discovered the 'underlying truth'?

Interestingly, Huxley, having exposed the multiplicity of types of truth, seems also to have been drawn to reconciling them. Reductionism – the idea that truths of various kinds can be 'reduced' to truths of a particular kind, as in the view that ultimately everything can be explained by the laws of physics – is one method of reconciliation, although Huxley was never tempted down that road. Reductionism denies multiplicity completely. Mysticism reconciles different truths without denying them; it simply postulates a higher truth that can only be apprehended by direct intuition. Huxley would slowly work through this idea throughout his working life, and would give it full expression in the chapter 'Truth' of *The Perennial Philosophy*. For the moment, it seems to have attracted him, while repelling his sceptical intellect.

Education

When different sources of knowledge are found equally compelling, issues are raised about what sorts of education one should provide. It is no surprise that Huxley was interested in education. His mother, father and grandfather, in their different ways, were all educationalists. His brother Julian had been invited to create the Department of Biology at the Rice Institute at Houston, Texas (now Rice University). Aldous himself had been a schoolmaster too. Right until his final days, Huxley had things to say about education.

As shall be discussed in later chapters, the quality of Huxley's ideas on the topic didn't always justify the number of his interventions. In his early works, his general position was that most approaches to education were misconceived, and that the education system was being twisted to perform acts of social engineering for which it was ill-suited. This was a corollary of his scepticism, expressed more satirically than seriously. In *Antic Hay* Gumbril's career as a schoolmaster is brought mercifully short by his decision to patent his pneumatic trousers. This is a good thing, given that 'I have come to the conclusion ... that most people ... ought never ... to be taught anything at all ... What's the use of teaching them anything except to behave well, to work and obey?' This is obviously an exaggerated caricature, and indeed even those for whom teaching is a vocation have been known to utter such sentiments after a difficult Friday, yet in essence it is not far from Huxley's settled view. In his more sober essays, he still insisted that:

> knowledge has had its most disastrous effects on the minor men, on the rank and file ... [It] has brought with it restlessness, uncertainty and the possibility of rapid and incessant change in the conventions of art.

('The Pierian Spring', *Along the Road*)

and that:

> I have no belief in the power of education to turn public-school boys into Newtons (it being quite obvious that, whatever opportunity may be offered, it is only those rare beings desirous of learning and possessing a certain amount of native ability who ever do learn anything).

('Views of Holland', *Along the Road*)

But most of his satire at this time tended to be along the lines of 'I had the disadvantage of the best education the English public school system could devise' – the sort of joke which the rich and droll still make nowadays. For instance, in *Along the Road* he complains that he was the 'unfortunate victim' of Eton ('Views of Holland') and lingers over 'the extreme inadequacy of my education' ('Conxolus'). At this stage, he declined to draw out any wider social implications; as we shall see in later chapters, he was not to remain so circumspect.

Popular culture

If the high culture to which a public school could give access was no solution to the dilemmas of the age, still Huxley was no cultural relativist. He retained throughout his career a scathing attitude to popular culture, first expressed in his story 'Eupompus Gave Splendour to Art By Numbers' which appeared as early as 1916, and which was often connected with an ill-disguised contempt for the masses, and a rather racist attitude to the burgeoning jazz culture of black Americans. Another aspect of this contempt was that he found it hard to understand 'the masses' as consisting of autonomous individuals; he usually explained the fact that they watched or listened to rubbish by arguing either that the ruling political class wanted to divert them from the 'real' issues, or that tedious mechanised work would drive people to seek easy solace in jazz and the movies, or that the inadequacies of serious modern artists provided no viable alternative. He was particularly suspicious of the shared influence between popular entertainers and the experimental artists he so often lampooned in his books. In an essay on 'Popular Music' from *Vogue* in 1924, later reprinted in *Along the Road*, he opined that:

> Barbarism has entered popular music from two sources – from the music of barbarous people, like the negroes, and from serious music which has drawn upon barbarism for its inspiration … If Rimsky-Korsakoff had never lived, modern dance music would not be the thing it is.

Only sometimes did he enjoy himself in the cinema or the dance hall. In an essay of 1925, 'Where are the Movies Moving?' he confesses that his favourite dramatic hero is Felix the Cat, and enjoys the visual puns of the Felix cartoons. He prophesies that the medium would lend itself to what he calls 'super-realism' – an Anglicisation of 'surrealism', then a newly minted artistic movement in France (André Breton had published the *Surrealist Manifesto* the previous year).

The advertising industry was another career-long bugbear. Although he treated it more seriously in his later works, he was always alive to its absurdities, akin to the 'quack's patter at the fair' (as he wrote in 'Advertisements' from *On the Margin*). In a fine series of comic scenes in *Antic Hay*, the advertising man Boldero designs a campaign around Gumbril's pneumatic trousers; given the impossibility of selling them using sex, he ponders branding them instead as an innovation – no matter that they are ridiculous, they are *new* and novelty sells. He tries using medical gobbledegook. And, to paraphrase Dr Johnson, the last refuge of the ad-man is patriotism, as in Boldero's slogan 'English trousers filled with English air, for English men'. Yet the comedy prefigures the more trenchant commentary of years to come. 'Advertisements' expressly connects democracy, education, the oppression of the masses and the degradation of language.

All was negative, nothing sacred, everything apparently of value undermined, yet ultimately Huxley was either unwilling or unable to remain cynical. In his early work there are precious few hints of any positive vision, but the second half of the decade saw his first faltering steps to save the world from the advertisements and jazz.

3

Vitalist, 1925–30

Life

Aldous and Maria set off in September from Italy, bound for India. Both of them seem to have spent the journey, which lasted the best part of a year, lusting after Mary Hutchinson, and both wrote her letters comic and erotic in turn. Maria was torn, not wishing to leave Matthew behind (he was after all just five). Nevertheless that is what she decided to do; even when he fell ill, though worried, the Huxleys did not return to Europe.

Huxley's opinions of his destinations as expressed both in personal letters written at the time and in the public narrative which he called *Jesting Pilate*, were completely inconsistent with many of his later beliefs. He did not enjoy India, and his view of the locals was at times frankly racist. It was not, of course, unusual before the 1980s for an Englishman of any class to express racist or anti-Semitic views casually and privately, although in public life it was assumed that all subjects of the British Empire should receive equal treatment from the authorities. In the 1920s, this ambivalence was extremely common. Whether or not one accepts and forgives those unpleasant expressions which were common currency at the time, it has to be admitted that in this respect Huxley completely failed to transcend his milieu.

Yet his analysis of India was keen, and his contempt for imperialism powerful. The Huxleys travelled widely across the subcontinent, with extended stays at various places, and were impressed by some of the politicians of the All India Congress. Aldous was unreasonably rude about Gandhi, a man he later came to admire greatly, in his private correspondence.

After a long stay in India, the Huxleys continued to tour the East, going to Burma, Malaya, Singapore, Java and the Philippines. On the ship, Maria helped engineer an affair between Aldous and a Romanian princess, whom she disparaged mercilessly in letters to Mary Hutchinson. The Huxleys crossed America via Los Angeles and Chicago, half bedazzled, half appalled by the Jazz Age. Three significant meetings took place: with Charles Chaplin in Hollywood (Aldous was entranced by his brilliant conversation); in New York with the satirist H.L. Mencken, whom Huxley had long admired and corresponded with; and with Anita Loos, the author of *Gentlemen Prefer Blondes*. Huxley loved her work and had written her a fan letter; they got on famously. Meanwhile, he was lauded as a celebrity intellectual; one radio address reached an audience of forty-three million.

Upon their return to England in June 1926, Maria went on to Belgium to be reunited with Matthew. Extraordinarily, Aldous stayed with Mary Hutchinson for several weeks before following Maria.

Although Chatto renewed his contract for another three years for an increased advance of £650, and *Two or Three Graces* did well, there were signs of a backlash against Huxley the wunderkind; Thomas Hardy felt him clever yet unmemorable, a view backed up by an interview in the *Daily Sketch* portraying him as unsentimental and cold, clever but unfeeling, a weary, cynical chronicler of a hostile world. Huxley himself had encouraged this picture with self-portraits such as Denis Stone, Gumbril and Chelifer, but he was outgrowing this personality. Unbeknownst even to Huxley the long journey in unfamiliar cultures pushed him away from ironic disconnection; one can see in *Jesting Pilate* the germination of a desire to make a positive contribution, and a belief that it might be possible.

Huxley finally collected Matthew from his grandparents in Belgium in August, and the family now went to Cortina d'Ampezzo in the Dolomites. He had read André Gide's new novel *Les faux-monnayeurs* (*The Counterfeiters*), and was impressed by its ambition. His new work was to attempt a similar comprehensiveness, describing the complexities of human and social life in all its myriad aspects; a person is a collection of molecules, a structure of cells, a being defined by its social roles, a psychological individual, an artist, the subject of art, an economic agent. Huxley wanted to express the chaotic interactions between all these levels as eloquently as his brother Julian, by now a famous scientist. *Point Counter Point* would be one of his greatest works, but at first he struggled in his mountain chalet.

With a new Itala six-cylinder two-litre, the Huxleys did more driving around, meeting Pirandello in Padua, Arnold Bennett in Cortina, and Lawrence again in Florence; neither Lawrence nor Frieda found Aldous, who was disheartened by his struggles with the novel, very lively or interesting. After months of pleading from Aldous and Maria, Mary Hutchinson finally came to Cortina in March 1927 to continue the *ménage*, but her 'official' lover Clive Bell was suspicious (her husband St John Hutchinson seems rarely to have been consulted). Soon after, Huxley decided to return to England, reintroducing himself to intellectual society and plunging into politics, for example spending more time with H.G. Wells, for whom he had not previously shown great warmth.

The death of Maria's grandfather occasioned a visit to Belgium, where Huxley was deeply impressed with the elaborate Catholic ritual. To some correspondents he emphasised the farcical aspects, but his philosophy of the wearisome condition enabled him to treat as independent the spirituality of a religious occasion or ritual from the ramshackle nature of its implementation (certain passages in *Jesting Pilate* had exploited the same incongruity). From Belgium the Huxleys went back to their beloved Forte, where they now had a wide circle of Italian friends, and invited the Lawrences, who grumbled, and the Morrells.

July saw the completion of a collection of socio-political essays, *Proper Studies*, which gave him some relief from *Point*

Counter Point. Christmas found them in Florence as guests of the Lawrences. Lawrence had a healthy scepticism about both Huxley's talent and his ideas, although he appreciated his kindness and (sometimes) his conversation. By now, it would be no exaggeration to say that Huxley was under Lawrence's spell. He simply found Lawrence enormously stimulating, enjoying his affirmation of life and instinct as an antidote to his own dry, introverted intellectualism. Lawrence was also very fond of Matthew and Maria – she typed the manuscript of *Lady Chatterley's Lover* (promptly if inaccurately) and, unused to the intricacies of Nottinghamshire profanity, would casually drop some of the more robust epithets into general conversation, to Lawrence's horror. He did, however, suspect Maria of being over-fond of money, and didn't like her driving everywhere (he was opposed to cars).

Christmas was followed by three months in the Vaud in Switzerland with the Huxleys, the Lawrences and Julian and his wife Juliette in close proximity; D.H. eventually grew frustrated at the dry, scientific discussions between the Huxley brothers about the genetic improvement of mankind, but once more there was serious consideration of his ideas for a community on a ranch in New Mexico; Aldous and Maria thought of spending six months there.

Back to London, and the manuscript of *Point Counter Point* was finally delivered, hopelessly late, in May 1928. More travels followed, but not to New Mexico; the Huxleys took a house in Suresnes near Paris in June, and then almost immediately took off for Forte once more, via yet another stay with the Lawrences in Switzerland, before returning in the autumn, when Huxley was able to bask in the acclaim for his new novel (fewer people liked it than liked the earlier satires, but the greater ambition of his art was admired). The Suresnes house was decorated by one of Maria's brothers-in-law, a professional painter, while the success of the novel meant they were able to afford armchairs specially adapted to Aldous's extra-long legs – and when they bought their pride and joy, a 1929 touring Bugatti two-seater, they customised that for Aldous as well. A brief visit to London in January 1929 brought Huxley's first meeting with Gerald Heard, a polymath, writer and conversationalist who would become one of the Huxleys' greatest friends. On this cold January night, their talk went on until one o'clock in the morning, whereupon the two, having missed their buses, had to walk several miles to their respective homes.

June found the Huxleys together with the Lawrences in Forte once more, grumbling about the philistinism and violence of Mussolini's fascist government. There were tensions – the Huxleys were seriously concerned for Lawrence's health and frustrated at his refusal to see a doctor about the tuberculosis which was slowly killing him. Lawrence for his part felt fussed over.

During this time Huxley was working on the stories which later made up *Brief Candles* and a series of essays which became *Do What You Will*, the intellectual counterpart of *Point Counter Point*, and with those out of the way, the Huxleys spent Christmas in Suresnes – Aldous met James Joyce in Paris, although it was not a meeting of minds – hopping over to London to supervise a dramatic adaptation of his novel. Although it flopped, he immensely enjoyed the experience of the theatre, however, and immediately wrote the first of his not-very-good plays, *The World of Light*.

Yet in February 1930 they were on the move again, to the south-eastern corner of France where word had reached them of Lawrence's deteriorating condition. They stayed with him and Frieda for ten days, until his death on 2 March. They were devastated, Maria particularly, while Aldous was moved by the extinction of Lawrence's powerful spirit. Later that year, Huxley accepted the job, without remuneration, of editing Lawrence's letters; his introduction[1] remains an important source critically and biographically, and in one of his most heartfelt pieces of writing describes how 'to be with Lawrence was a kind of adventure, a voyage of discovery into newness and otherness'. There was a valuable spin-off from this project; Huxley visited Eastwood, Lawrence's birthplace in Nottinghamshire, which became a longer exploration of the unfamiliar territory of the North of England, spawning a couple of interesting essays about class and geographical divides which appeared in *Nash's Pall Mall Magazine* in 1931.

They remained in the South of France, within days of Lawrence's death taking a home in Sanary-sur-Mer overlooking the sea, and began to mix with the elite colonists of the area, including Edith Wharton. They made a few enemies as well; Cyril Connolly and his wife, firm admirers, came to stay, got on incredibly badly with Maria in particular, and then spent much of the 1930s vitriolically criticising Aldous's work. Yet a crucial period for Huxley was beginning. *Point Counter Point* had made him a public figure. The mellowing effect of the ageing process had devalued the satirical point-scoring and mockery which had made his reputation. He had always been an implicit moralist, although so far an entirely negative one. He was now thirty-six; he wanted a positive philosophy. His first steps in this direction had been missteps, over-dependent on Lawrentian vitalism. Now Huxley, deprived of his guru, needed to work out for himself where to go.

Work

Jesting Pilate (1926)

Along the Road had been a collection of essays linked by the theme of travel, but *Jesting Pilate*, which narrates the Huxleys' round-the-world trip, was his first unified travel book proper (it was constructed from a series of pieces collectively entitled 'Diary of an Eastward Journey', published in *Nation* in London and *Bookman* in New York in 1926). The narrative structure, with the greatest detail on the Indian leg of the tour, highlights the magpie nature of Huxley's mind. Events often take a back seat to his impressions and thoughts.

The title is a quotation from the seventeenth-century philosopher Francis Bacon, from his essay 'On Truth': 'What is truth? said jesting Pilate, and would not stay for an answer.' A major theme of the work is the multifarious nature of experience, with a relish reminiscent of the sixteenth-century essayist Montaigne in the diversity of people's experience. Huxley enjoys the culture shock of hearing a Muslim talk of Sicily as a Mohammedan country 'cruelly ravished from its rightful owners, the Arabs'. 'To travel is to discover that everybody is wrong.'

The tour from India to America gave him an opportunity to measure a highly spiritual society against a materialistic one. He found much to admire, and more to appal him, in each, but his write-up of his experiences leaves the reader in no doubt that when faced with the alternate realities he approved of addressing man's material needs before his spiritual ones (even if he did *not* approve of focusing entirely on materialism in the absence of any kind of spiritual depth – in fact, much of his later career was spent trying to sketch the correct balance between the two). India left him thinking that it needed 'more materialism and not, as false prophets from the East assert, more "spirituality" – more interest in this world, not in the other'.

Proper Studies (1927)

Proper Studies is another carefully chosen title, adapting Alexander Pope's line that 'the proper study of mankind is man', and signalling the new socially engaged Huxley's investigations of politics and society. The witty and erudite essays on history, art and literature are far fewer in number, replaced by a series of pieces (almost all specially written) exploring the politics of his recent thinking, including (a) his lack of faith in democracy, based on his experience of American society, (b) his axiom that there is an infinite variety of valid subjective understandings of the world, (c) his conviction that many problems in the world followed from unquestioned simplistic assumptions, and that only hard-headed but open-minded thinking could lead to effective government, and (d) his faith in intelligence, science, art, technology and technocratic planning to uncover the best policies for a conflicted and often unjust and violent society.

Dashed off between January and July 1927 in-between spells of writing *Point Counter Point*, the work is not yet clearly thought through, and as a political manifesto is unsatisfying (Huxley himself came to look upon it with disfavour[2]). It was influenced by the ideas of Italian sociologist Vilfredo Pareto (1848–1923), according to whom the distribution of income was constant across societies, which implied that democracy was a sham – it could change or improve nothing. Any attempt to improve a social system artificially would meet opposing forces that would restore the previous equilibrium. His socioeconomic psychology appealed to Huxley, who used it in 'The Idea of Equality' to demolish the myth that all men are equal. This was symptomatic of the book's weakness; he argued against a straw man, and ignored alternative and reasonable types of egalitarianism, such as the promotion of equal rights, equality before the law or social democratic ideas about partial and progressive redistribution of wealth.

His assumptions that few people sustained sufficient interest in politics to support properly democratic institutions, and that our evolutionary inheritance cannot be overcome (i.e. that human nature cannot be changed), entailed that political systems based on ideal behaviour (such as communism) were untenable, and in fact the best systems were hierarchically based, with a small elite dominating the many. Who were the elite to be? Ideally their composition should be determined using intelligence testing (even of voters) and examinations. Huxley's interest in Pareto would continue for some years.

Point Counter Point (1928)

In Gide's *Les faux-monnayeurs*, the character Edouard announces that he is writing a novel, and explains his theory.

> I should like to put everything into my novel. I don't want any cut of the scissors to limit its substance at one point rather than at another. For more than a year now that I have been working at it, nothing happens to me that I don't put into it – everything I see, everything I know, everything that other people's lives and my own teach me …

Point Counter Point was a conscious attempt by Huxley to extend his art and to express a serious artistic, psychological and political truth. In this it was only partially successful, but it remains one of the most important works of the 1920s. Using Greville's 'Chorus Sacerdotum' as epigraph, it is an attempt to portray in literature the multiplicity of experience and significance, as for example when Marjorie Bidlake muses upon her unborn child: 'what had been a blob of jelly within her body would invent a god and worship; … what had blindly lived in her as a parasitic worm would look at the stars, would listen to music, would read poetry'. Art, as one character points out, moves one 'precisely because it's unadulterated with all the irrelevancies of real life'; Huxley wanted to achieve the effect of art while including all the irrelevancies and inconvenient truths of life. Characters act and interact, and events are intertwined with others that conflict or contrast; these are the counterpoints that have to substitute, in real life, for meaning.

The opening set piece, a musical evening at the Tantamounts' house, is a case in point; we are introduced to the characters while Bach's Second Orchestral Suite (described both in terms of the sublime music, and in physical terms as the product of the scraping of lambs' intestines) plays in the background. The characters are less than lovable. Lucy Tantamount is another of Huxley's Circe figures, another Nancy Cunard, almost entirely vicious. Spandrell, like Coleman in *Antic Hay*, consciously rejects the idea that moral standards apply to him with the sort of contemptuous philosophy associated with Baudelaire, but once more the tone is darker. Whereas Coleman is the source of slapstick comedy, Spandrell is permanently negative, depressed and depressing, sordid in his seductions and ultimately failing to gain any interesting sensation from the gratuitous murder he commits (another borrowing from Gide, who explored the idea of motiveless crime in some detail in *Les caves du Vatican* and *Les faux-monnayeurs*). Burlap is a sanctimonious hypocrite, whose resemblance to Huxley's former employer John Middleton Murry was strong enough to cause the latter to contemplate challenging the former to a duel (this, given Huxley's blindness, would have been a decidedly Burlapian thing to do). Even the minor characters are ineffective and deluded; the fascist leader Everard Webley (often erroneously taken to be a caricature of Oswald Mosley, who was still a mainstream Labour Party politician at the time of writing[3]) is a pompous and sinister fool, while the revolutionary Illidge is clearly incapable of overthrowing capitalism (the only thing he overthrows is himself as he tumbles down a long flight of stairs in full view of everyone at the Tantamounts' soirée).

Further darkening the tone, Huxley includes the usual unsparing sketch of himself as a major character, but with fewer redeeming features than Denis Stone or Francis Chelifer. Philip Quarles is emotionally retarded, withdrawn and uncaring. According to Lawrence, *Point Counter Point* caused a minor rift between Aldous and Maria, not because Quarles's wife contemplates an affair with the charismatic Webley, but because the Quarles's little boy, who, like Matthew Huxley (upon whom he was modelled[4]) falls ill while his parents are on a round-the-world trip, actually dies from meningitis in one of the most morbid twists in the Huxley canon.

As with *Those Barren Leaves*, Huxley tries to leaven the heavy atmosphere with a positive philosophy, exemplified in the character of artist Mark Rampion. Rampion leads a harmonious existence, balancing all his various needs and desires; he works, he is clever, yet is not arid like Quarles. He is talented (unlike Lypiatt from *Antic Hay*, who shares Rampion's critical faculties but cannot paint), and has a happy, loving marriage. He is human, but doesn't try to transcend his humanity, as he tells Burlap, Quarles and Spandrell at enormous length. He has life right, knows he has, knows everyone else has it wrong, and is not shy of pointing it out.

Lawrence recognised himself as the model for Rampion, and correctly if bluntly informed Huxley that 'your Rampion is the most boring character in the book – a gas-bag. Your attempt at intellectual sympathy!' Neither, sadly, was Gide impressed. In his journal for 18 March 1931 he confided, 'Went as far as page 115 with great effort. Unreadable.'

Do What You Will (1929)

Do What You Will, a collection of essays about half of which were published for the first time, tries to integrate Lawrentian vitalism with Huxley's theory of infinitely diverse subjectivity. The title, this time from Blake, once more cleverly signals intent:

> Do what you will, this world's a fiction
> And is made up of contradiction.

The politics of *Proper Studies* is ditched in favour of engagement with Life with a vitalist capital 'L'. The result is an unlikely product of Huxley's typewriter; he ticks off some of his favourite writers and thinkers for their anti-Life philosophies. Swift, Baudelaire and Pascal find themselves on the receiving end, even though, for instance, few writers were more Swiftian than Huxley in their recognition of unpleasant realities, the unrealism of romance and the symbolism of morbidity and bodily corruption.

At least the theme is authentic Huxley. The opening essay, 'The One and the Many', argues that those eras in which monotheism has held sway are the most barren and materialistic; monotheistic religions such as Islam, Judaism and Protestantism are products of the desert, inimical to healthy society. Polytheistic religions, on the other hand, thrive in spiritually and culturally rich times, whether of the classical civilisations or those of the modern-day Mediterranean, where Catholicism draws upon several deities including Jesus, the Holy Spirit, the Virgin and the Saints, who even if they are not of equal status with God at least provide diversity in the heavenly host. In the essay on Pascal, he argues that men ignore the fact that each is 'a colony of separate individuals' because of their hatred of life and an 'intellectually vicious love of system'. He (Huxley) himself tries, if not always successfully, to 'be sincerely all the numerous people who live inside my skin' – neatly restating the wearisome condition in Lawrentian terms.

Modern industrial civilisation prevents most people from expressing all the personalities within themselves, while popular culture engenders passivity. On the other hand, revolutions and other violent struggles for power are driven by crude idealisations of justice, righteousness or fairness. This half-religious, half-psychological interpretation of politics was to grow in prominence in Huxley's work in later years, and ultimately would lead to his easy assimilation of mysticism, religion and politics. At this point in his career, however, he still saw religion as an obstacle to appreciation of the many layers of reality.

Brief Candles (1930)

Huxley's final collection of uncollected short stories, *Brief Candles*, like *Mortal Coils* took its title from a metaphor for life taken from a Shakespeare soliloquy about the transience and contingency of existence, this time Macbeth's 'tomorrow and tomorrow and tomorrow' speech. The allusion to meaninglessness is perhaps a sign that the influence of Lawrence was receding; in this collection Huxley put forward few positive solutions to life's problems. As with most of his collections, *Brief Candles* is structured around a specially written and accomplished novella. 'After the Fireworks' questions the role of the writer in creating illusions; an older novelist begins a relationship with a young impressionable girl. Huxley once more uses the symbolism of decay and mortality to puncture delusions of romance; their affair founders when the novelist falls ill as a result of their sexual excesses.

The three shorter stories are also successful. 'Chawdron' (the only other specially written piece) is the tale of a financier captivated by a girl who has mystic experiences. 'The Claxtons' satirises the totalitarian instincts of the earnest sandal-wearing vegetarian faddist type. In 'The Rest Cure' Moira Tarwin is so entranced by Italy that she grows away from her husband, and begins a relationship with the son of her hotel-keeper, which ends tragically but ironically.

Thought

Huxley was unimpressed with India and the Far East in his first visit, but the round-the-world trip still catalysed his intellectual development. The diamond-bright, diamond-hard sceptic of the early 1920s, who had trashed all common sources of value, commenced a search for his own. The problem (in the West at least) was materialism; value could not be discovered by the scientist or the accountant, but people 'have not trusted their own immediate and intuitive conviction' that things have non-material value. However, the unsentimentality that had made Huxley a brilliant satirist in the early 1920s produced a positive programme that on occasion makes for ugly reading.

Meaning, value and the influence of Lawrence

Many people make the mistake of trying to deduce value from facts about reality. At this time, Huxley began to think about the reality that underlies Greville's 'wearisome condition of humanity', and crafted it in the most repellent terms. If value comes from reality, he implied, then it won't be noble or uplifting. He revelled in the ugly, the unpleasant, the unjust and the meaningless, and castigated those who wished to make sense of the world – this was just childish, he wrote in 'Swift' (in *Do What You Will*), 'like all such protests, from the fairy story to the socialist's Utopia'.

The world has no meaning, and no point. In *Jesting Pilate* he pointed out that we do not speculate over why cows or elephants are there; why should we wonder about ourselves? 'There is as little *reason* why we should be here, eating, drinking, sleeping, and in the intervals reading metaphysics, saying prayers, or collecting dung.' Furthermore, reality was too complicated to encompass in its totality, as he argued in many places, for example in 'Varieties of Intelligence' (in *Proper Studies*) and 'Swift', where he said that 'Life is not a cross-word puzzle, with an answer settled in advance and a prize for the ingenious person who noses it out. The riddle of the universe has as many answers as the universe has living inhabitants.' This is the philosophical underpinning of *Point Counter Point* – there is no coherence to be had, beyond the pleasure of extracting some harmony from completely independent musical lines.

Yet although this was very similar to the characterisation of the wearisome condition with which Huxley's readers were already familiar, the meaninglessness was given a Lawrentian twist. Meaning wasn't absent; it was just that 'The best answers are those which permit the answerer to live most fully, the worst are those which condemn him to partial or complete death', a canonical Lawrentian criterion.

Those Barren Leaves had tentatively raised the possibility that there might be some source of value beyond the discredited ones of the past. In his next novel, *Point Counter Point*, Huxley specifically introduced for the first time a representative of a positive value unambiguously endorsed by the author. Mark Rampion is a whole person. We are shown in flashback his courtship and happy marriage. He finesses the wearisome condition by living at all levels to the full. So what if men and women are mere animals? In that case, in Rampion's words, 'to be a perfect animal *and* a perfect human – that was the ideal'. Or, as Huxley wrote in his own voice in 'Pascal', the ideal man's

> fundamental assumption is that life on this planet is valuable in itself, without any reference to hypothetical higher worlds, eternities, future existences … [T]he end of life … is more life, that the purpose of living is to live.

One should live for the moment, planning as little as possible, by instinct, 'naturally'. The Greeks had got it right; their polytheistic pantheon reflected the multifarious aspects of man and his relations with the world. Even now, according to Huxley, the people with the best attitude to life were still those from the relaxed South of Europe.

Rampion's criticism of modern society is devastating, and plainly endorsed by the author. Religion, science, technology and industry have wrecked everything. 'It's Jesus's and Newton's and Henry Ford's disease.' Religion makes us live for a future paradise, and neglect the business of the here and now. Science and technology make us believe we can control the world rather than celebrate and enjoy it. Industry turns us into quasi-machines, ignoring our own destinies to lead wage-slave lives of utter tedium. If only, he wrote in 'Wordsworth in the Tropics' (from *Do What You Will*), we could be both Jekyll, intellectual, sensible and boring, *and* Hyde, instinctive and physical, as required, keeping those two sides of our personalities alive but separate.

Huxley himself had problems following the Lawrentian ideal. The major difference between them, both intellectually and temperamentally, was over science. Lawrence abhorred the dry dissection and classification of the material world which he understood science to be, and he realised Huxley remained within that scholarly scientific tradition not only by inheritance from his grandfather, but also by temperament. For his part, Huxley couldn't help but be suspicious of what he considered Lawrence's anti-intellectualism. In short, Huxley was several parts Jekyll to a dash of Hyde, and would drive Lawrence mad with his elegant and reasonable conversation – and he recognised this. In *Point Counter Point* Philip Quarles appreciates Rampion's genius but can't find it within himself to let go his inhibitions and follow him. He can't even tell his wife of his great affection for her. He is addicted to intellectual pursuits, but he knows they are not enough; Lawrentian vitalism is essential to give ideas a purchase on the world.

If the lesson of modernity that there was no intrinsic meaning to reality was unleavened by Lawrentian vitalism, the result was merely negativity and ultimately nihilism, as shown by the morally bankrupt Spandrell. Spandrell is a true modern, but because his mind is untempered by Rampion's humanity he has given his life over to vice. He enjoys corrupting a young girl, and revels in his own remorse. But eventually even he finds such evils unsatisfying, and he is driven to increasingly extreme diversions; he plots with Illidge to murder the fascist Webley. The murder only achieves an increase in the popularity of Webley's party, and in the end Spandrell deliberately tips them off that he is the killer. In a typically Huxleian juxtaposition, he is playing Beethoven's late A minor string quartet on his gramophone while Webley's thugs beat him to death. Beethoven's last sonatas and quartets had always inspired Huxley and he describes poetically the accompaniment to Spandrell's murder: 'Then suddenly there was no more music; only the scratching of the needle on the revolving disc.'

The natural world

For Huxley, nature was a subject for nostalgia. Although he lived much of his life in natural or non-urban environments, he rarely wrote much about them in his fiction. This may have been for the very simple reason that his poor eyesight prevented him from seeing them. Instead, rapturous flashbacks to lost childhoods contained loving descriptions of nature when he would describe mellow Edwardian days growing up in light, and peace and beauty.

However, he became more interested in nature intellectually, as a source of value. In later life, he would become an ardent environmentalist, and we see the first inkling of that at this time. In *Point Counter Point*, admittedly, the dangers of over-exploitation are expressed through the mouth of the rather absurd Lord Tantamount, whose obsession with phosphorus overwhelms the wider points. But the points *are* made. In answer to Webley's suggestion that money is the route to civilisation and progress, Tantamount responds: 'Progress! You politicians are always talking about it. As though it were going to last. Indefinitely. More motors, more babies, more food, more advertising, more money, more everything, for ever.' He concludes: 'You're upsetting the equilibrium. And in the end, nature will restore it.'

Meanwhile, Huxley also attacked those who sentimentalised or anthropomorphised nature. In 'Wordsworth in the Tropics' and *Jesting Pilate*, he developed a counterfactual thought experiment of how Wordsworth's pantheistic nature worship/philosophy would have developed had he been born in a tropical outpost of empire. 'The Wordsworthian adoration of Nature has two principal defects. The first ... is that it is only possible in a country where Nature has been nearly or quite enslaved to man.

The second is that it is only possible for those who are prepared to falsify their immediate intuitions of Nature.'We can detect the outlines of a Gaia-like philosophy that nature has its own Pareto-style equilibria which we disturb at our peril, as the mechanisms of adjustment are unlikely to be very congenial to human survival. 'A few months in the jungle would have convinced him that the diversity and utter strangeness of Nature are at least as real and significant as its intellectually discovered unity.' Huxley argued that we should celebrate, rather than neutralise, Life and nature, but equally we should not sentimentalise or falsify them either.

Education: the Dalton Plan

An immediate example of Huxley's new engagement with politics and policy following his return from India was his investigation of new methods of education. After the rather lazy satire on teaching systems in *Antic Hay* and elsewhere, in late 1926 he published a piece in *Vanity Fair* about the Dalton Plan (this being the first of many faddish schemes and plans which grabbed Huxley's enthusiasm over the years). Under the title 'How Should Men Be Educated?' he makes the point that the question cannot be answered; different people have different requirements, all of which would be catered for in a scientifically ordered state.

The Dalton Plan,[5] developed by Helen Parkhurst in the 1920s after philosophical differences with the Montessori philosophy, and still followed in a few schools round the world, reorganises schools so that individual learning outweighs class teaching. The child is given a series of assignments to be completed in a period of time, but decides him- or herself which studying to do when. The child therefore learns problem-solving and planning. Clever and not-so-bright children progress at the pace that suits them. Hard work is rewarded by attainment. Different children develop different skills.

Huxley contextualised the Dalton Plan in a chapter on 'Education' in *Proper Studies* where he lambasted uninspired teaching in large classes, which is of necessity intolerant and rigid. He also, surprisingly, lambasted inspired teaching in small classes too, because the clever teacher relieves the children of the necessity of finding out things for themselves. Daltonisation is the only solution. His criticisms of the universities ran along similar lines (indeed, have their echoes today); too many people there for snobbish reasons, or because 'a university is a delightful club for young people'. He approved of the Oxbridge system as the Dalton Plan *avant la lettre*.

Democracy

The ultimate aim of education is to train every person to 'fit into the place he or she is to occupy in the social hierarchy, but without, in the process, destroying his or her individuality'. The planned state would solve such problems as these, according to Huxley who tended to dismiss the problems that the planned state might *cause*. In his *Vanity Fair* essay on the Dalton Plan, he specifically contrasted the neat, planned state with democracy:

> we live in a democratic world. No scientifically ordered state, it is obvious, could be democratic; it would be aristocratic: the most intelligent would be the rulers. But we have universal suffrage; the vote of the half-wit is as good as that of the one-and-a-half wit.

Huxley was ambivalent about democracy. His view was not a million miles away from Churchill's famous quip that democracy is the least worst system we have, but he laid more emphasis on 'worst' than on 'least'. In *Jesting Pilate* he was pleased to affirm that his 'prejudices happen to be in favour of democracy, self-determination, and all the rest of it'. Yet in 'Political Democracy', from *Proper Studies*, he wearily admits that:

> the defects of political democracy as a system of government are so obvious, and have so often been catalogued, that I need not do more than summarize them here. Political democracy has been blamed because it leads to inefficiency and weakness of rule, because it permits the least desirable men to obtain power, because it encourages corruption.

The first two points may be arguable, but the third seems completely false. Democracies tend to be less corrupt than dictatorships, because, in effect, more people have to be corrupted.

Huxley certainly opposed rule by the rich, yet he refused to subscribe to the idea that the poor should rule; he imagined that they would rule badly, and wanted the intelligent to rule. This is what he called 'aristocracy' 'in the etymological sense of the term' – in other words, 'ruled by the best of its citizens'. True aristocracy, he maintained, could only be implemented in states that were *more* democratic than the current one, as:

> in the contemporary democratic state it is possible for the worst to govern and for the best, if they happen to be born in unfavourable surroundings, to be distorted by disease and hunger, handicapped mentally by inadequate education, and wasted throughout an entire lifetime on unsuitable work.

Hence Huxley's ideal at this time was really something like a modern meritocracy with greatly enhanced equality of opportunity.

Greater democracy was fine, but its success was contingent on other changes in society. Huxley was not keen on the democratic ideal of universal suffrage. It was a 'manifestly absurd state of affairs' that anyone could stand for Parliament, and therefore that anyone, even certified idiots, could be qualified to be a cabinet minister.

His solution was to make sure that only those with a mental age of fifteen could vote, via a 'fairly stiff' intelligence test. Like many of his characters – for example, Walter Bidlake in *Point Counter Point* – Huxley could not trust, or be enthusiastic about, the masses he wanted to help. The problem was exacerbated by the fact that they would not help themselves, but preferred to vegetate in the 'world of silliness and criminality' portrayed on the movie screen. In 'Silence is Golden' (from *Do What You Will*) he described his first visit to the talkies. It is fair to say that he did not enjoy it:

> I comforted myself a little with the reflection that a species which has allowed all its instincts and emotions to degenerate and putrefy in such a way must be near either its violent conclusion or its no less violent transformation.

Eugenics

Huxley's elitism was reflected at this time in his interest in eugenics. He assumed that this would be uncontroversial in a scientifically planned society, and he rarely criticised the basic assumptions underlying them. His fullest treatment was in 'A Note on Eugenics' in *Proper Studies*, in which he tried to imagine what would happen if the ratio between 'dull-witted' and 'strong, intelligent, and active' people was altered. He specifically refused to consider how this may be done, and so didn't get into the minefield of policy to do with sterilisation and 'stud farms' of Nobel Prize winners, with which he was later to have such satirical fun in *Brave New World*.

How should we define the inferior ones, usually derided as feckless, idle, incompetent? Some eugenicists drew the line on racial grounds, while others assumed that class was the determiner, but most tried to avoid the charge of prejudice. Class prejudice in particular was hard to dispel, because in anyone's theory the inferior types, whoever they were, were likely to be worse-educated and poorer. It was very easy to appear to suggest that all poor people with inadequate educations were inferior, even if this was not one's intention. Major Leonard Darwin, son of Charles and a leading eugenicist, proposed to use income as a proxy for fitness so that the eugenic project was, in Huxley's words, 'the systematic discouragement of fertility among the ill-paid and its encouragement among the well-paid'. This seemed to Huxley to be the most appropriate practical method of making the division.

Eugenics assumes that the inferior people breed more prolifically, so that the proportion of inferiors would tend to grow over time. In 'What Is Happening to Our Population?' in 1934, Huxley pointed out that 'twenty-five years ago there were between four and five half-wits to every thousand of population; today there are between eight and nine' and concluded that '*we may look forward in a century or two to a time when a quarter of the population of these islands will consist of half-wits*' (Huxley's emphasis). Whether or not one accepts the value judgement in the definition of inferiority, the eugenic assumption turns out to be false. Certainly birth-rate declines as education and income increase, but this applies to the children of the ill-educated and poor as well as the better-off; there is no genetic component. One could more easily solve the problem of the supposedly prolific breeding of the inferiors by improving their social and economic status, rather than preventing them from breeding. In any case, it is not clear that, however one defines them, the proportion of 'inferiors' has grown in European society.

Huxley's 'Note' drew an ambivalent conclusion. Deterioration would be bad: 'the breed of superior men will be altogether eliminated; and the process is likely to be hastened by a revolt of the numerically powerful sub-man'. But equally, because:

> the socially efficient and the intellectually gifted are precisely those who are not content to be ruled ... a state with a population

consisting of nothing but these superior people could not hope to last for a year … If the eugenists are in too much of an enthusiastic hurry to improve the race, they will only succeed in destroying it.

In later work, however, his enthusiasm for eugenics would receive greater emphasis.

Huxley: anti-Semite?

Much about Huxley's philosophy at this time was distinctly unpleasant. Given what would happen in the 1930s, his anti-Semitic remarks of this period have not unnaturally drawn the attention of many readers. However, his attacks on Judaism, which are most prominent at this time, have to be seen in the context of his general attacks on all organised religion, which, although they were both more common and more virulent at this point, continued right up to the 1960s. His essay 'The One and the Many' from *Do What You Will* is characteristic.

If what Renan [Ernest Renan, a nineteenth-century French historian and philosopher often criticised for anti-Semitism] says about the sterilizing effects of pure monotheism be true (as I think it is) how are we to explain the fact that the races of Europe have not sunk, since their conversion, to the level of those deplorable Semites, among whom their historian could find no art, no science, no philosophy, no politics, none of those activities, in a word, which justify men in taking a certain pride in their humanity? The tree shall be known by its fruits.

Strong stuff. Can it be defended? Clearly there is a strong core of prejudice which cannot be argued away. One might mention four factors in partial – only partial, let it be emphasised – mitigation.

First, in this particular context, Huxley was arguing for the social value of polytheistic religion (not that polytheism is true, only that it has a better effect on society and culture). He was suggesting that the Greeks had the best attitude to metaphysics, that anticipated and adapted itself to man's wearisome condition. It was an argument to which he often alluded throughout his career, borrowing the terminology of a distinction between Hellenic culture (polytheistic, tolerant) and Hebraic culture (puritan, moral) from Matthew Arnold. Mankind is a multiplicity. He argued that Judaism was chiefly responsible for the import of monotheism to Europe, via the Christianity that it spawned.

Second, Huxley's attitude to Judaism in particular changed with the rise of the Nazis. His anti-Nazi credentials, as we shall see, are unchallenged. Overt anti-Semitic remarks disappeared from his published prose.

Third, Huxley disliked all organised religion. In the same essay on monotheism we are told that 'Calvin's Geneva is another open sewer'. In 'Baudelaire', also from *Do What You Will,* 'stupidly consistent' Puritanism received the full force of Huxley's rhetoric: 'The puritan was and is a social danger, a public and private nuisance of the most odious kind.' Huxley did not write often about Islam, but his occasional references were also unflattering.[6]

In general, he grew less sarcastic and abusive about the major religions after his own religious conversion in the 1930s, but never relinquished his belief that they were responsible for much of the misery and unhappiness in this world; he tended to prefer mystical sects rather than mainstream orthodoxy. Nonetheless, one must admit that his hostility to Judaism (and Islam) came from a position of ignorance.

Fourth, in many cases Huxley's 'Jewish' characters have been identified as such only by critics with little or no guidance from the text. For instance, Chawdron (from *Brief Candles*) is a businessman without taste whose first name is Benjamin – that is all the evidence Huxley provides, although many have concluded from this that he is a Jew. Sometimes there is more to say; in *Brave New World*, Mustapha Mond is named after Sir Alfred Mond, the Jewish chairman of ICI, and has a big hooked nose.

Virtually all the anti-Semitic references in Huxley's published works are uttered through the mouths of characters who do not express the authorial voice, most of whom are villains or otherwise unpleasant. Huxley uses anti-Semitism as a well-known social indicator of an intolerant and unsympathetic character. In his letters and occasionally his essays, however, Huxley certainly gives voice to very similar sentiments – most notably when he fulminates against popular culture, particularly the movie industry where 'you depend on Jews with money'.[7]

Given these four factors, even quite determined inquisitors have found it difficult to convict Huxley of genuine anti-Semitism.[8] He did not approve of Judaism's tenets, or indeed those of any organised religion. Of the two classical sources of Western culture, he preferred that of Greece and Rome to that of the Bible. He lazily assumed that Jews were well represented in the world of industry and business of which he did not really approve. He was not shocked by the expression of anti-Semitic (or other racist) sentiments. He certainly defended the Jews, as best he could, through his writings after the rise of the Nazis.

4
Prophet, 1930–2

Life

The next couple of years saw Huxley shuttle between Sanary and London, gradually leaving behind the influence of Lawrence, with whom in truth Huxley had very little intellectually or temperamentally in common. Lawrence's appeal, based so much on his 'oppressively visceral' presence (Huxley's phrase), was always unlikely to survive. Lawrence was quickly replaced in the role of Huxley's guru by Gerald Heard, who shared with Huxley an all-encompassing interest in knowledge, a desire to push intellectual boundaries and a love of no-holds-barred conversation. Heard's interests included science, particularly evolution, psychical research, early history, theology and philosophy; though now forgotten, he was then a prominent public intellectual and broadcaster, and helped ease Huxley into a public role.

Huxley became more engaged politically, and concerned with the reality of life. Whether an Eton and Balliol man of those days could understand the common run of most people's experiences in the absence of the sensibility of a George Orwell (Huxley certainly did not have such a sensibility) is perhaps moot, but Huxley understood that, disarming critics by admitting, for example, that he had more in common with the Dean of Durham Cathedral than with the miners to whom he had just delivered a lecture. He listened to, and was appalled by, a Parliamentary debate on the depressed economy, which he felt was constantly harking back to bygone ideas. He travelled around what he called 'alien Englands', visiting docks, mines and factories and exposing this hidden world to his upper-middle-class readers. He began to delve into the philosophy of Henry Ford, and continued to develop his backward-looking critique of the harshness and loudness of the clothes, music and cinema of the time.

By now Huxley was so celebrated that it would have been difficult to avoid him. His play *The World of Light* opened at the Royalty Theatre in March 1931 (closing shortly afterwards, despite decent reviews), while May saw his final book of poetry, *Cicadas*. He delivered the Thomas Huxley Lecture (rekindling his admiration for his grandfather's literary style and scientific acumen in the process), and his journalism was syndicated across the Hearst newspapers. A new book of essays, *Music at Night*, appeared, and he began his long career as a broadcaster in earnest, with lectures, debates and conversations on the BBC.

February 1932 saw the publication of his masterpiece *Brave New World*, in which he sketched a future in which all our preferences were satisfied, gerrymandered by scientific techniques; it sold very well (13,000 copies in the first year in the UK) and cemented the reputation that Huxley had built with *Point Counter Point*, leading Chatto to renew its generous contract with yet another increase in his annual advance. Perhaps because of its implicit criticism of consumerist materialism, the new novel initially sold less well than expected in the US.

Still more minor works appeared in 1932. Another play, *Now More Than Ever*, a satire on the career of the 'match king' and fraudster Ivar Kreuger, was written but never performed.[1] Long thought lost, the play turned up in time for the Huxley centenary and was published in 2000; it is perhaps the most solid of Huxley's dramatic works. His edition of Lawrence's letters arrived, as did an anthology of poetry, *Texts and Pretexts*. A new novel was begun, but the pressure to follow the previous two blockbusters gave him writer's block; he made little progress and the book stalled. He also felt the lack of a positive vision in his work once more; in *Point Counter Point* he had borrowed Lawrence's ideas while *Brave New World* had worked brilliantly as a satire. It was clear what Huxley was against, but he still had not set out clearly what he was *for*. The next few years were spent searching once more for that positive vision.

Work

Vulgarity in Literature (1930)

Vulgarity in Literature appeared in the *Saturday Review of Literature* in September 1930, and as a limited edition pamphlet a few weeks later, and has usually been reprinted as an additional piece in *Music at Night*. Although it is padded out to meet a requirement of length, and although its flippant tone somewhat contrasts with his more socially committed work of this time, it is an interesting piece as an expression of some aspects of Huxley's artistic credo. 'Art ... is also philosophy, is also science. Other things being equal, the work of art which in its own way "says" more about the universe will be better than the work of art which says less.'

Huxley had often been accused of vulgarity himself, in his discussions of sex, disease, corruption, death and romance, and he admits that 'the aristocratic pleasure of displeasing is not the only delight that bad taste can yield'. Literature 'should investigate the still obscure relations between the mind and the body'. This means describing 'the vulgarity of this having to walk and talk; to open and close the eyes; to think and drink and every day, yes, every day, to eat, eat and excrete'. In fact, says Huxley, literature becomes *really* vulgar when real life is clothed in misleading bromides and idealisations, as when the death of Little Nell in Dickens's *The Old Curiosity Shop* is turned into a ludicrous fugue of emotion.

There are interesting discussions of Poe, Dostoyevsky and Dickens, and the few pages he devotes to Balzac suggest how his never-written book on that author might have gone. In his discussion of Balzac's novel *Séraphita*, Huxley's paradoxical fascination with mysticism resurfaced: 'Literature about the inexpressible ... a London fog, but coloured pink.' Yet though his head tells him it is nonsense, he cannot withdraw his gaze from 'a strange alternation of light and darkness: light to the limits of the possibly illuminable and after that the darkness of paradox and incomprehensibility'. It even becomes quasi-political: 'Mysticism brings with it the decay of authority. The process is, to some extent at least, reversible; the decay of authority leads to mysticism.'

Music at Night (1931)

Music at Night appeared in mid-1931, prefiguring a number of themes from *Brave New World* (fourteen of the twenty-five essays were specially written, and of the others, only one, 'Those Personal Touches', appeared prior to 1930). It explores the limits of the science of the time, and Huxley is able to think through various futures and possibilities, good and bad. His interest in eugenics reappears in less equivocal form in 'Boundaries of Utopia', where he expressly calls for 'deliberate breeding and selection' in order that progress should continue. 'On the Charms of History and the Future of the Past' ended with a hint of the inevitability of 'a Machiavellian system of education, designed to give the members of the lower castes only such instruction as is profitable for society at large and the upper castes in particular that they should have'.

Much of the collection is a continuation of themes from *Vulgarity in Literature*. 'Art and the Obvious' complains that high art has left certain topics that loom large in human life (love, the beauty of nature, the close link between mother and children) to popular art which gives 'deplorably beastly expression to the obvious'. 'Tragedy and the Whole Truth' argues that the artistic exploration of the 'whole truth' characteristic of modern writers such as Proust, Gide, Hemingway, Lawrence and Kafka, has caused the temporary eclipse of specific and 'chemically pure' art forms such as tragedy. Other pieces discuss poetry, science and music as means of expression.

In perhaps the most important piece in the book, 'Wanted: A New Pleasure', Huxley argues that the importance of pleasure to modern society and the modern economy has turned it into a commodity. He makes his first tentative suggestion about the use of drugs as artificial stimuli for world-weary modern man, and ironically suggests that a drug that left no effects of addiction or withdrawal would mean that 'all our problems … would be wholly solved and earth become paradise'. The nature of that paradise would be explored in depth in his next substantial work of fiction.

Brave New World (1932)

The title of *Brave New World* is taken from Miranda's speech at the end of *The Tempest*. She has been stranded on an enchanted island with her father, the magician Prospero, and has grown up since the age of three with only the deformed monster Caliban for company. When a party of not-terribly-impressive sailors and villains are brought before Prospero, Miranda is amazed and bursts out:

> O wonder!
> How many goodly creatures are there here!
> How beauteous mankind is! O brave new world
> That has such people in't!

Huxley's title communicates the grimness of the world he has created, together with the hope and optimism born of ignorance with which it is viewed by its denizens.

Jesus, Mahomet and the Buddha have been discarded in the brave new world. The spiritual leader is now Henry Ford, known ubiquitously as 'Our Ford'. The year is 632AF – that is, After Ford, the time dating from the invention of the Model T, the first mass-produced and mass-consumed car. All the Christian crosses have had their tops removed to make them into 'T's. While Huxley takes deadly accurate aim at Fordism, mass production and the science of efficient management named Taylorism after its pioneer Frederick W. Taylor, he also pokes fun at other aspects of modernity that irritated him. For instance, the inhabitants of the brave new world do not know why, when 'Our Ford' dealt with matters of human psychology, he would refer to himself as 'Our Freud', delivering paeans to communal living, and arguing that all attempts at exclusivity, including family life and monog-amous love, led to pain and distress. Huxley always had a healthy disrespect for Freud, and in later life was reported to have crossed himself piously whenever Freud's name was mentioned at a psychology conference he was attending.

In this world, human procreation has been entirely mechanised. Babies are incubated in bottles, and human sexuality liberated from the demands of child-rearing. Both men and women are rampantly promiscuous, while words like 'mother' and 'father' are dirty and embarrassing. Pleasure is the aim of everything, and society is organised so that people are spared the frightening anticipation of harm. Even babies are fed immediately they cry to avoid the feeling that 'lurks in the interval of time between desire and its consummation'. A non-addictive drug, soma, is widely available to ensure maximal cheerfulness, and is taken whenever any kind of worry or depression threatens.

Care has been abolished; solitude is frowned upon; illness and death happen out of sight, in special hospitals. Attitudes are formed via hypnotherapy; from an early age, sleeping children are played tapes of soothing voices reciting moral precepts ('liking what you've *got* to do'). The mechanisation of childbirth has allowed pre-birth categorisation; the people of this future are pre-programmed with greater or lesser intelligence and physical characteristics, and divided into Alphas (for advanced managerial tasks), Betas, Gammas, Deltas and Epsilons (produced in large numbers for repetitive unskilled labouring). Hypnotherapy is used to condition economic behaviour, connecting pleasure with consumption for the consumerist command economy.

The main protagonist of the book is a misfit, an Alpha-plus psychologist called Bernard Marx who has been stunted (rumour has it) by alcohol leaking into his container during gestation. Despite hypnotherapeutic exhortations towards promiscuity, he is deeply attracted towards, and envious of the lovers of, the pneumatic (to borrow the slang of the sixth-century AF) Lenina Crowne.

Bernard wants to explore the regions of the world that are not organised along Fordist lines, and takes Lenina on a fateful trip where they discover Linda, a marooned Beta who has been forced to live the humiliating life of a savage, with monogamous relationships and child-bearing. Her son John has an inquiring mind and a compendious memory for Shakespeare, quotations from whom he uses to provide a commentary on what he finds. Bernard and Lenina bring Linda and her son back to civilisation; the novelty briefly makes Bernard a celebrity, but John Savage (as John becomes known), Linda and Bernard come to sad ends, now inevitable outsiders in both the ultra-modern and the savage society. Mustapha Mond, one of the ten World Controllers, reasserts order.

Texts and Pretexts (1932)

Huxley's next project was the pleasing anthology *Texts and Pretexts*, in which he gathered together poetry illuminating philosophical issues. Although it is a minor work, it remains a civilised ramble through some of the finest expressions of thought, differing from other anthologies by the philosophical commentary accompanying them. Huxley was able to illustrate some of the ways in which human wisdom can be expressed at the very limits of language, using words to suggest rather than express deep truths.

Texts and Pretexts follows the axiom of *Vulgarity in Literature*: 'Art … is also philosophy, is also science.' It is also an early corollary of the important principle governing Huxley's later career that individual goodness has to precede political progress; in his anthology he in effect argues that great poetry holds more lessons than more direct and declarative political works.'As the influence of religion declines, the social importance of art increases. We must beware of exchanging good religion for bad art.' Huxley defends himself against the charge of frivolity of producing a poetry anthology in the slump, fiddling while Rome burns: 'perhaps Rome would not now be burning if the Romans had taken a more intelligent interest in their fiddlers'. Life imitates art, and the position is worse for modern man because 'the conceptions in terms of which men interpret their experience have been altered by science out of all recognition'. Decoding and translating timeless truths from verse situated in time is part of Huxley's purpose.

The book is divided into over forty mini-essays linking eclectic poetical offerings with commentary; there are chapters on love, man's place in nature and various aspects of the *comédie humaine*, as well as other striking pieces, including 'Vamp' (which comments on verse by Drayton with a single paragraph describing and dismissing the Nancy Cunards of this world), 'Money' and 'Nonsense'.The poets included will already have been familiar to Huxley's readers; as well as Greville's 'Chorus Sacerdotum', the French symbolists and Dante are well represented (although unfortunately for the monoglot not translated into English), as are the Romantics and the metaphysical poets.

Thought

After the Lawrentian detour of the late 1920s, Huxley reverted to satirical type and forgot about the ideal man. He still sought after an affirmative philosophy; for instance in *Texts and Pretexts* he anthologised the finest poetry explicitly as a kind of antidote to the political problems of the day. But the ideal man was now rejected as a feasible possibility – the one basically good person in *Brave New World*, Bernard's friend Helmholtz Watson, feels his life and work are empty but doesn't do much about it and doesn't intrude very far into the action, while the most effective character, powerful Alpha-plus Mustapha Mond, is the consummate smooth villain. Indeed, Huxley went so far, in *Texts and Pretexts*, to opine that the twentieth century had *no* ideal.

Huxley's works in this period were still concerned with value; where do values come from, and why do they disappear? Which are important, and which merely flim-flam? Although at this point he reached no settled conclusion, more lines of thought emerged that would be enlarged upon and extended in his later works.

The irrationality of value: body and mind

One theme was his total lack of interest in social movements and forces. In a contribution to a symposium on 'If Christ Should Come Today!' in 1932, he opined that 'His ministry, if he were now to return, would be in the world of individual souls', and concluded that – given the current impossibility of resting a metaphysical system on God:

> the only adequate reason for a transcendental ethic is to be found in the human psyche. Certain states of being, felt to be supremely desirable, can be reached and held only by those who practise a certain kind of behaviour.

The new Jesus would require 'a fundamentally humanistic philosophy'. The task of making this idea compelling and attractive was hard but not necessarily impossible; gradually, as he thought more about the problems of the 1930s, it shaped Huxley's thought.

States of mind were clearly connected to states of the body, so it seemed to Huxley that ethics and moral philosophy had to take into account the physical embodiment of moral agents as well as their psychology. In *Texts and Pretexts* he explicitly connected value and physiology in a way that would become central to his thought. 'There are values which persist, because there is a physiology which persists and, along with a physiology, a mental structure.' He pointed out that this broad correlation was not new; poets had always identified the spleen, or bile, as the cause of human misery ('they may have been wrong about the offending organ').

He believed that ideas survived, in many if not all cases, not because of their intellectual content or humane repercussions, but for entirely contingent reasons to do with our physical make-up, and would later explore this view in some depth. In *Brave New World* ideas are implanted not using reason, but via mindless slogans during sleep, while Mustapha Mond argues that human illness and the ageing process are what bring awareness of, and a need for, God. Health and happiness, however artificially induced, were the best prophylactics against religious sentiments.

In 'On Grace', in *Music at Night*, he argued that heredity had at least as great a part to play in the development of moral attitudes and status as environment; this was the great problem with communism as it was understood at the time:

> For though we can prevent one man from having more money than another, we cannot equalize their congenital wealth of wits and charm, of sensitiveness and strength of will, of beauty, courage, special talents.

Salvation depends on inborn qualities: 'in other words, it is the result of favouritism and predestination'. That is not to say that

Huxley thought that heredity was destiny. Environment was important. He was also fully prepared to accept that exceptional individuals could transcend all their influences by transformative acts, often in politics or the arts. He refused to believe Shakespeare was a 'product' of anything, whether his genes or the environment in Stratford in 1564.

Engineering people

The 'nature vs. nurture' argument had deep roots in the human and psychological sciences, but Huxley also appreciated earlier than many that, because most if not all of the factors underlying human behaviour were bodily mechanisms and chemical interventions, it would in theory be possible to reproduce their effects with technology. In other words, the advantages and disadvantages of heredity could be copied and redistributed technologically. Huxley's other brilliant realisation was that this did not necessarily mean that everyone would become *Übermenschlich*. His studies of the urban environment,[2] of industry and the factories in which Taylorism and mass production predominated, his extensive reading in the literature of the industrial revolution, especially Dickens and Disraeli, and his long friendship with Lawrence, all helped him realise that life in the big, smoky, grey, dark industrial cities would oppress the human spirit. One had to sublimate one's desires to the infinitely specialised task one was given; one was turned into a specialist in a tiny nameless part of a large industrial or manufacturing process. The work was mindless, and so mindlessness was wanted; entertainment became etiolated; music became rhythm and noise; buildings became boxes; literature became sentiment. If people thought too hard, or appreciated finer things, they would work less well.

How would the authorities react if they had the technological means to mimic or control heredity? To Huxley it was obvious. They wouldn't try to improve people – they would instead, as the Taylorists had done on the factory floor, fit people to the niches they needed to fill. And if that meant churning out idiots incapable of questioning their lot, then so be it.

Standard economics dictated that people's choices be influenced by financial incentives; Huxley realised that people could actually be engineered to choose socially desirable ends. Their choices, determined largely through heredity, would be part of their genetic 'blueprint'. They would not be formed freely as a result of an unfettered life; autonomy would disappear. Yet choice would *be* free; there would be no coercion; action would be voluntary. Into this nightmare world came John Savage, but such a world would not be a nightmare for its inhabitants. Only for Savage, and for the reader, is the horror of this brave new world visible.

Ideology: the individual, the masses and the planners

There is some debate as to whether Huxley was warning of a potential future in *Brave New World*, or using the parable of the future to criticise the society in which he lived. The novelist Michel Houellebecq has argued for the latter,[3] that the world Huxley had prophesied was simply free-market capitalism and democracy allowing their victims to satisfy their preferences without hindrance. Nicholas Murray in reply argued that this reading misleadingly implied that Huxley endorsed the world he had created.[4] However, Murray seems not to have taken in Houellebecq's irony at this point. Huxley seems to have flip-flopped between the two positions – possibly to the point of inconsistency.

Morality, he believed, was the province of the individual, and larger forces merely amplified the effects of individual preferences. It follows from this that much if not all of the responsibility for bad government lies with the people being governed. Yet in *Brave New World* itself Huxley describes a command economy presided over by Mustapha Mond and his associates who deliberately keep knowledge of struggle, hardship, love and emotion from the populace to preserve an Edenic state of paradise without good and evil. Although Huxley is plainly of the opinion that Eden is not much cop, the implication of Mond's suppression of the works of Shakespeare (of which he, uniquely apart from John Savage, is aware) is that, faced with the examples of Juliet, Othello, Hamlet and Prospero, people would *not* make the choices that Mond had conditioned them to make. Huxley wished to use *Texts and Pretexts* to acquaint people with the glories of the best poetry in order to promote better thinking, which although the opposite of Mond's action, was justified by the same thinking.

Huxley cannot have it both ways – the horrors of the world he created are either the fault of planners, capitalists and the makers of anodyne popular art, all of whom work to suppress the best influences on humanity, or alternatively the consequences of people's free (authentic, unconditioned) choices. The novel works as a powerful indictment of modern society if interpreted in the latter sense.

Furthermore, when we consider the potential solutions to the dilemma posed by *Brave New World*, Huxley also seems caught between the potential of planning and the mobilisation of the individual conscience. High culture presented positive modes of existence which were denied to the mass of people because of lack of education, interest and access. Economic and technological conditions were key factors in that denial. Yet science could provide analyses of how to improve the human condition, and it appeared possible to Huxley and many other intellectuals of the 1930s to use technocratic plans if only governments could face the truth and find the energy to develop them.

He did not wish to redraw society along ideologically perfect lines. His preferred option was to use the human sciences to tell us exactly what the grain of human nature was, so that the plans could go with it. The point of *Brave New World* was to warn us about the ease with which square pegs, to borrow one of Huxley's most common proverbs, could be fitted into round holes. As Bernard flies over the savage reservations, Huxley contrasts the rough Mexican landscape with the implacable electrified frontier fence, 'uphill and down, across the deserts of salt and sand, through forests … march[ing] on and on, irresistibly the straight line, the geometrical symbol of triumphant human purpose'. The skeletons of animals are scattered along its length.

High art and the vulgar

Huxley was beginning to come to terms with his distance from the great mass of people, and realising that it did not preclude political action. In his play *Now More Than Ever*, he put the following speech about the wretched victims of injustice into the mouth of the communist Walter Clough:

> Why are their minds so limited and personal? Always, me, me, you, you; never an idea or a generalisation. And then that awful indifference and resignation! The way they put up with intoler-able situations! Nobody has a right to be resigned to slums and sweated labour and fat men guzzling at the Savoy. But damn them, they *are* resigned … But all the same, I believe it is possible to love one's neighbour even though one may have very little in common with him.[5]

Huxley's response to his disconnection was to examine art as a means of improving society, and also as a key variable in explain-ing why it had reached such a low. His prejudices were well-known; he hated jazz and the movies, and wrote eloquently about Beethoven and Piero della Francesca. At the beginning of his career these were merely semiotic markers, the badges of two different tribes. In the 1920s, art was a part of the Bloomsbury inheritance. *Of course*, when one wrote a novel, one's characters were painters and novelists, because that's who one knew. *Of course*, when one wrote an essay, one illustrated it with examples from Shakespeare and Piero, because they formed the understood and shared cultural background between author and audience.

As Huxley tried to adapt his thought to a wider audience and a more tangible set of problems, he began to unpick the mechanisms and assumptions underlying great art, and to defend vigorously its claims to importance. In *Texts and Pretexts*, at first sight a 'mere' anthology, he actually constructed his deepest defence of the canon of Western thinking. *Brave New World* had implied that science could, and maybe would, steamroller everything in the absence of other sources of genuinely meaningful value. The sceptical Huxley found it easier to deconstruct the claims of science in his masterpiece, but strained for a positive answer. As he explained in *Texts and Pretexts*, he found at least one answer in art, which shapes the thoughts and feelings we have, and 'if the art we like is bad, then our thinking and feeling will be bad'. And if that is so in a society, 'is not that society in danger?' Understanding political, social, psychological and philosophical issues via the finest works of poetry can only do good. 'They also serve who only bother their heads about art.'

There is demand for art, argued Huxley in 'Art and the Obvious'. In the modern era, mechanisation, which has made working life so unsatisfying and stupefyingly dull, has created a space which has been filled by leisure, which includes art, literature, music and film. More art requires more artists, more artists mean more bad artists. These artists follow the masses rather than lead them; they would rather say what people want to hear, than challenge convention: 'The present age has produced a hitherto unprecedented quantity of popular art (popular in the sense that it is made *for* the people but not – and this is the modern tragedy – *by* the people).'

Life and art, for Huxley, are symbiotic. So, for example, vulgarity in art will tend to produce vulgarity in life, but the converse is also true. A vulgar society will produce vulgar art. What is vulgarity in this context? In *Vulgarity in Literature*, Huxley argues that it is anaesthetisation of the serious 'stuff' of life such as death, sex and disease with romance and idealisation. It is literally an an-aesthetic.

Maybe a perfect technocratic world will do away with the need for art, or change art by changing the needs of its audience. Mustapha Mond thought so, in a famous passage.

> You can't make flivvers [small inexpensive cars like the Model T] without steel – and you can't make tragedies without social instability. The world's stable now. People are happy; they get what they want, and they never want what they can't get. They're well off; they're safe; they're never ill; they're not afraid of death; they're blissfully ignorant of passion and old age; they're plagued with no mothers or fathers; they've got no wives, or children, or lovers to feel strongly about; they're so conditioned that they practically can't help behaving as they ought to behave. And if anything should go wrong, there's *soma*.

Mond's attitude was absolutely opposite to Huxley's instincts. The chronicler of the wearisome condition finds the subject matter of art across all types of life. In his T.H. Huxley Memorial Lecture he argued that all verbal communication was literature to some degree, albeit that some types of experience lend themselves to the stylistic innovations of the artist more than others. In his essay 'Tragedy and the Whole Truth', from *Music at Night*, he highlighted the realism in the passage from Book XII of the *Odyssey* when Odysseus relates how he and his men land on an island after six of their companions have been killed by Scylla. They first satisfy their thirst and hunger, and then weep for their companions, after which they have a pleasant and restorative sleep. This is a complete portrayal of life; grief coexists with hunger and exhaustion, and no one of these emotions ever takes complete hold. However, in tragedy the focus is on the grief, in the absence of the other cravings. It may lead to profound and beautiful poetry or prose, but it is unfaithful to life. Similarly in *Texts and Pretexts* Huxley berated those nature poets who are happy describing the beauty of the natural world, but omit the supernatural evil and ugliness that one also encounters. Tragedy may indeed be the most wonderful of all the genres, but it is not the whole truth, and there is art to be made from the whole truth, however prosaic it may seem.

Huxley endorsed those writers and poets, like Chaucer, Burns, Fielding and of course Shakespeare, who were able to place tragedy in its rightful place, as a sometimes overwhelming but never all-encompassing part of life. Even Lawrence struggled to live up to this requirement; in his introduction to the letters Huxley pointed out that Lawrence's fine instinctive grasp of the world did not compensate for his complete lack of understanding of, and interest in, science.

In passing, we might note that in one respect at least, Huxley's work had become *less* realistic and all-encompassing. One unfortunate side-effect of the success of *Brave New World* as a novel of ideas was that women became increasingly marginal in his *oeuvre*. His wife, lovers and female friends were important to him throughout his life, and his early works, particularly *Crome Yellow*, had very prominent roles for women to play. No doubt this was partly because these works were *romans-à-clef* which featured the strong characters with whom he was in contact, like Nancy Cunard, Ottoline Morrell, Dora Carrington and Dorothy Brett. As he drifted away from the Garsington circle, so did the women gradually drift out of his novels; there were still many female characters in *Those Barren Leaves*, for example, but by then the men were doing most of the talking.

Brave New World, however, was an out-and-out philosophical parable. Abstracted away from actual events and characters to varying degrees, the important ideas were associated with the male characters. In *Brave New World*, the two women, Lenina Crowne and Linda, are pneumatic, promiscuous and slightly dim; the main dialectic of the talk and the action concerns the progress and fates of John Savage and Bernard Marx, with some good scenes with Mustapha Mond. Lenina's fate is basically irrelevant to the novel, a bit of comedy. This tended to be the case with Huxley's novels, which all concerned ideas rather than real people, from then on (at least until the unsuccessful *The Genius and the Goddess* in the 1950s, and to a lesser extent his final novel *Island*). Women were now more likely to appear as nymphomaniacs, mistresses, potential conquests or wives (sometimes all four). Unsurprisingly, few of these ciphers stick in the mind; perhaps only the voracious Mrs Thwale in *Time Must Have a Stop* is fully successful even in Huxley's own unambitious terms.

Huxley was also very clear about the importance of tradition for art, and was very scathing about those modernists who wanted to commence afresh with steel, machinery, movement, concrete, glass and lethal weaponry. Modernity in Huxley's view all too often led to passivity, uniformity and sterility. In his 1930 essay 'Puritanism in Art', he complains that the über-modernist architect Le Corbusier 'would compel us all to inhabit a mixture of greenhouse and hospital ward, furnished in the style of a dentist's operating chamber'.

In *Brave New World* he expressed his love of tradition by laying out a society that had eradicated it, concentrating on its unsympathetic Corbusian architecture. The 'squat' building whose description opens the novel is *only* thirty-four storeys, while every block, apartment, hospital and official building in which significant action occurs is described with great relish. Yet he also enjoyed playing with the concepts and genres of art, reasoning (correctly, we now realise) that technology would allow formal barriers to be breached. His description of the 'feelies' – movies with added touch sensations – anticipates the immersive simulated environments we now call virtual reality. Another rather wonderful idea, not yet implemented in the real world (though one yearns for it), is the scent organ:

> playing a delightfully refreshing Herbal Capriccio – rippling arpeggios of thyme and lavender, of rosemary, basil, myrtle, tarragon; a series of daring modulations through the spice keys into ambergris; and a slow return through sandalwood, camphor, cedar and new-mown hay (with occasional subtle touches of discord – a whiff of kidney pudding, the faintest suspicion of pig's dung) back to the simple aromatics with which the piece began.

5

Pacifist, 1933–7

Life

The first half of 1933 saw the Huxleys on their second life-changing tour, also destined to become a thoughtful and controversial travel book in the manner of *Jesting Pilate*. This time the destination, possibly suggested by Lawrence's example, was Central America – the West Indies, Venezuela, Belize, Guatemala and Mexico, and once more the Huxleys were disappointed. They didn't like their English middle-class, middle-aged fellow passengers on their cruise liner, and were unimpressed with West Indians as well; Huxley's letters at the time are sometimes amusing but undeniably snobbish about the whole thing. Mexico seemed to him dark, violent and brutal: 'can't share Lawrence's enthusiasm'.

Yet *Beyond the Mexique Bay* describes an important moment, in Barbados, where he witnessed a very ordinary domestic scene with two West Indian women at their household chores. There was nothing of importance about the scene, yet it mysteriously held 'a quality of extraordinary alienness and unfamiliarity'. He describes it movingly; not for the last time, Huxley was learning the significance of the minor, the quotidian. He remained scathing about the 99.5% of 'stupid and philistine' people, but this was increasingly tempered with liberalism and compassion.

The journey also contributed to the evolution of his political beliefs. His exploration of Mayan ruins led to a discussion of the nonsense of racial difference as a political concept. The Central American leg of the tour confirmed his growing belief that psychology, not politics, was the chief determining factor in the problems of the age, as well as making obvious the exploitation of sweated labour to provide commodities for the European and American markets.

The final leg took them to New York, where they dined with H.L. Mencken, before returning early to Europe following the sudden death of Aldous's father. Sanary was by now a magnet for Germans fleeing the new Hitler regime, including the great novelist Thomas Mann. Huxley, though annoyed about this influx of 'a rich selection of Jews', retained a tolerant and anti-fascist public position (the erosion of the public/private division characteristic of today's political world had not yet occurred in the 1930s; Huxley would find no contradiction between remarks in private correspondence and his liberal political outlook).[1]

In late 1934 the Huxleys acquired a base in England, a flat in the Albany, a famous residence near Piccadilly, London, with a literary reputation dating back to Byron's stay there. Meanwhile, his public persona was growing: the first full-length study of his work appeared in 1935,[2] and his public appearances at well-meaning conferences increased in frequency. In Paris, he attended, and was thoroughly bored by, a conference to discuss the future of the European spirit, while Welwyn Garden City was the venue for a conference on sexual reform. One writers' conference in Paris, where he warned about the dangers of propaganda, turned out to be secretly sponsored by communists, a fact not lost on the FBI.

Huxley's open mind was becoming less tolerant of rationalism and 'common sense', and he began to flirt with obscure medical techniques and cultish religious ideas at about this time. The year 1933 found him on the recently devised Hay diet, which keeps 'acidic' and 'alkaline' foods separate, while taking yoga breathing exercises and cultivating the friendship of the psychiatrist Charlotte Wolff, who investigated the potential of the hand for diagnosing psychological problems. This coincided with a period of ill health, including serious insomnia that struck in 1934 and

1935 which threatened his work. In the end, he met and was impressed by F.M. Alexander, an Australian therapist whose Alexander Technique re-educates posture and physical movements so that the whole organism functions correctly. The Huxleys went on to embrace enthusiastically the ideas of J.E.R. McDonagh, whom Alexander had recommended, which meant a special diet and regular colonic irrigation. Whether fortuitously or not, the insomnia disappeared and his blood pressure fell.

Huxley was approaching a type of crisis. He remained able to function throughout, though it was a difficult time for him and Maria. The transition in his persona from destructive satirist to committed individual (he now argued that 'there is nothing inherently absurd about the idea that the world which we ourselves have so largely constructed can also, if we so desire, be reconstructed on other and better lines'[3]) was painful, and slowed by Huxley's need to rethink his position rigorously from first principles. The insomnia was possibly a function of this stress,[4] and its easing coincided with three mutually reinforcing developments in his thought. First, Huxley began to explore mystical religion in more detail, and with more sympathy; the influence of Heard was beginning to emerge.

Second, his political position hardened around opposition to what was widely felt to be the coming war. In October 1934, Dick Sheppard, charismatic canon of St Paul's Cathedral, published a letter inviting men to write him a postcard pledging to renounce war and never to support another. Sheppard's plea earned him 80,000 postcards within a year, one of which was sent by Huxley. On the back of this impressive public support, Sheppard formed the Peace Pledge Union (PPU) in 1936, which at its height boasted 130,000 members (after it had finally opened to women). Prior to the original appeal, Huxley had been thinking hard about peace, but was prevaricating; he had turned down a request earlier in 1934 from the novelist Storm Jameson to write a chapter for a book she was editing on pacifism. Heard's influence on Huxley was crucial, and by 1935, he was prepared to devote time and energy not only to writing (one contribution was to write the PPU's first pamphlet), but also to activism. He chaired the PPU's Research and Thinking Committee, and also accepted the presidency of an anti-fascist pro-peace cultural movement called For Intellectual Liberty.

Third, he rejected the *Proper Studies/Do What You Will* authoritarianism in favour of a more paternalistic model which fitted better with his elitism and his liberal democratic instincts. Mysticism connected with his ideas about the psychological causes of political malaise, and he began to suggest that spiritual exercises and the reformation of individual life could be the solution. This did not go down well on the left, which considered that unconditional pacifism was untenable; resistance to fascism would need the threat of violent retaliation as a last resort. His PPU pamphlet *What Are You Going To Do About It?* was attacked by Cecil Day-Lewis and Leonard Woolf among others for its abstract mystical vision and its perceived fatalism. Huxley would not move from his position that the worst way of tackling evil was to do another evil, a position he would eventually rationalise in *Ends and Means*. Largely as a result of this debate, Huxley and the politically engaged poets of the 1930s, W.H. Auden, Stephen Spender and Day-Lewis, would have a permanently low regard for each other's work and politics.

Huxley took up his projected novel once more in 1934, now seeing it as a way of exploring how the epochs of a life are related in some respects, unrelated in others. He was now four years behind delivery on his Chatto contract, and he began to worry about what might happen if the money from writing dried up. Nevertheless, by 1936, he completed *Eyeless in Gaza* incorporating his new outlook – an outlook that caused Maria to claim he was a 'new and unrecognisable person'. He took the opportunity to work though a few demons of his own; the suicide of Trev was narrated via the character of Brian Foxe. Less happily,

John Beavis was clearly an unflattering portrait of Huxley's recently deceased father, which drew an angry letter of complaint from his stepmother.

He was beginning to leave behind his artistic/literary circle, and to consort with practising scientists, psychologists and doctors, often on the fringe of scientific orthodoxy, whose direct engagement with the world he admired and increasingly wished to emulate. Yet the sense of crisis continued to overwhelm both Huxley and wider society. The passing pacifist moment was collapsing; despite amazingly strong support in Britain in the 1930s (incredibly, over 11,000,000 people responded, overwhelmingly positively, to a plebiscite sponsored by the League of Nations Union in 1935), the movement was split between those who were prepared to support a war to preserve freedom, such as Jameson and C.E.M. Joad, and those like Huxley, Heard and others such as Vera Brittain whose rejection of violence was unconditional. The chasm between these two camps could not be bridged, which led to incoherent responses to increased German and Italian aggression as the decade progressed. The public face of the pacifist movement was very dishevelled by 1939.

Huxley was not there to see it. Bored and frustrated by the decline of the PPU and For Intellectual Liberty, and depressed by political developments, he planned a long trip to the USA, prompted in part by a desire to ensconce Matthew in Duke University's medical school. The Huxleys were undoubtedly sad to let their residences in Sanary and the Albany go, and the title essay of Aldous's 1936 collection *The Olive Tree* is a paean to the Mediterranean life and culture that he sensed was slipping away. Even so, when Aldous, Maria and Matthew set sail with Gerard Heard and his partner Christopher Wood on the SS *Normandie* from London to New York in 1937, they did not have an inkling that their escape from Europe would be permanent.

Work

Beyond the Mexique Bay (1934)

Huxley's Central American trip was written up shortly afterwards as his third travel-themed book, *Beyond the Mexique Bay*, the title taken from Andrew Marvell's 'Bermudas', written in 1653. Marvell's poem had strong political intent, a puritan paean to the brave and devout mariners who explored and colonised the New World:

> He cast (of which we rather boast)
> The gospel's pearl upon our coast,
> And in these rocks for us did frame
> A temple, where to sound his name.
> Oh let our voice his praise exalt,
> Till it arrive at heaven's vault:
> Which thence (perhaps) rebounding, may
> Echo beyond the Mexique Bay.

Maybe Huxley was also poking a little fun at his fellow English passengers ('adolescents of five-and-forty abound') in the cruise liner sequences with which the book begins.

Yet after the early comedy, Huxley did discover, in chaotic Latin America, that war is the acme of all that is irrational in society and dangerous to mankind; of course, this is neither a terribly deep nor an original proposition, but it became a fundamental principle of Huxley's thought. The region, as part of the Spanish empire, knew long periods of uninterrupted peace, yet since independence had suffered dozens of wars and coups, each as irrelevant as the last. Most of the states were capitalist, but why would capitalists promote war, given that trade depends on stability? He hypothesised that nationalism constrains people 'by the emotional logic of an imported theology of hatred to renounce all their ties of blood and culture'. Huxley's response was still firmly elitist: 'Our need is rather for a World Psychological Conference, at which propaganda experts should decide upon the emotional cultures to be permitted and encouraged in each state.'

Irony tipped over into Huxleian tastelessness when considering the needs of 'the violent individuals of ... the imperialistic nations'. In a peaceful, civilised world, prevented by law from abusing 'wives, children and village delinquents', and 'lacking real Hottentots to bully' because of the cessation of war, such people would need a supply of victims to attack. 'In this context, it is not the colour of a posterior that counts; it is its kickableness.' These lapses in taste were always a self-conscious feature of Huxley's work; when, apropos *Ape and Essence*, George Orwell complained of Huxley that he was becoming increasingly sadistic 'the more holy he gets', and that he should have the courage to come out and say that 'if we took it out in a little private sadism, which after all doesn't do much harm, perhaps we wouldn't want to drop bombs, etc.' he was obviously unaware that Huxley had already said exactly that in *Beyond the Mexique Bay*.[5]

The travel diary remains interesting, with long digressions on war and the inhumane imbalances of the world economy. The main theme is the culture shock of the modern, educated European and the primitivism he encounters, and the clash of the decayed imperial Spanish culture with that of the poor Indians and West Indians. He lingers over his meeting with the head of the United Fruit Company's hospital, a Dr MacPhail, in Quirigua in Guatemala, 'one of the best and most charming of men ... the universal godfather of Guatemala'. By way of a tribute, a fictional but no less good Dr MacPhail turned up thirty years later in Huxley's final novel, *Island*.

What Are You Going To Do About It? (1936)

What Are You Going To Do About It? The Case for Constructive Peace was published under the auspices of the Peace Pledge Union.

Thirty-two pages long, this pamphlet was a reasoned development of the pacifist case in the face of a series of interventions from an 'intelligent heckler'. The aim was:

> to provide all those who *feel* that war is an abomination, all who *will* that it shall cease, with an intellectual justification for their attitude ... that what is called the utopian dream of pacifism is in fact a practical policy – indeed, the only practical, the only realistic policy that there is.

The first nine sections dismissed a series of objections to pacifism, beginning with the biological, before moving on to social, economic and moral ones; in each case the assumptions of those who reserved the right to resort to war were dismantled. The meat of Huxley's case arrived at the end. Section X suggested cutting the ground from under the warlike nations by recognising that Germany, Italy and Japan had a case for unjust treatment in the Versailles Treaty of 1919. The four 'great monopolistic powers', the British Empire, France, America and Russia, should call a conference to allow the unsatisfied powers to state their grievances, and should give ground. This would be risky, but no less risky than militarism.

The final section, XII, argued that if pacifism were to be effective, pacifists must be united.

> But there are unions and unions. The formation of yet another subscription-collecting, literature-distributing and possibly pledge-signing society is not enough. The Constructive Peace Movement must be ... a kind of religious order, membership of which involves the acceptance of a certain way of life, and entails devoted and unremitting personal service for the cause.

This surprising religious turn appalled the left. Huxley at this stage was not advocating any particular religious outlook (he often referred to the great ideologies of the day, communism and fascism, as religions too) but, impressed by the role of rites, prayer and meditation in providing moral strength and supporting the will, he thought Constructive Pacifists could benefit from them too. The sceptic is unlikely to be convinced.

> There is good evidence that the practice of some kind of spiritual exercise in common is extremely helpful for those who undertake it ... Meditation is a psychological technique ... [which] can be successfully practised by anyone who is prepared to take the necessary trouble.

To the modern reader (and most contemporaries), it seems unlikely as a mass political exercise.

For his part, as he had told Sheppard, Huxley believed the peace movement doomed unless it could become the core of an experiment in communal life. In the real world, people were not convinced. A Bradford peace worker, Margery South, complained that Huxley's Constructive Pacifism was fine for the 'bourgeois sentimentalist', but the group activities were 'absurd': 'I do feel it is the gap between the leaders of our movement and the ordinary person that is at the root of much of our lack of progress.'[6]

Eyeless in Gaza (1936)

Eyeless in Gaza is a flawed novel, not a major one in the canon of twentieth-century English literature, yet central for understanding Huxley's later thought. It was his most autobiographical work, incorporating, rationalising and transforming a number of incidents and situations from his life both recent (the travels in Mexico) and further in the past. Huxley was always ambitious for *Eyeless*, and ultimately it described the difficult conversion of a character not unlike the author from cynicism to engagement. The end was uncertain, the process hard (echoing the difficulties of writing the book), but the result uplifting. The title reflected the impotence of the pre-conversion protagonist, from Milton's description of Samson after his capture: 'eyeless in Gaza, at the mill with slaves'. Blindness (a real as well as metaphorical state for Huxley) and captivity at the mill symbolised separation from what is valuable in the world, and imprisonment in 'The dungeon of thyself.' And like Samson, the protagonist, Anthony Beavis is brought low by the wiles of a sensual woman, prior to a final redemption.

The book appears at first glance to be a complex formal experiment as the fifty-four chapters, each dated precisely, do not appear in chronological order, dislocating the reader and prompting him or her to look for parallels and discontinuities between the various stages of Anthony's life. However, the level of experimentation is not high; in fact, the book interleaves six sequences of events in linear order.

The first sequence takes place between late 1902 and early 1904, when Anthony goes through the trauma of the death of his mother and his father's remarriage to an unsuitable, greedy stepmother – small wonder Rosalind Huxley was unhappy. As well as these key emotional events, Anthony meets most of the major characters for the first time.

The second sequence, much longer, takes in Anthony's Oxford days between 1912 and 1914, where he neglects his schoolfriends for a fashionable set of aristocrats whom he really despises. One friend, Brian Foxe, is torn between his physical passion for a girl, and the impossibility of marrying her. Anthony's mistress Mary Amberley (another one of Huxley's vamps) challenges him to seduce Brian's girlfriend, which he does with relative ease. He intends to confess, but Brian finds out from her, and kills himself. Anthony is bereft with guilt and leaves Mary. He does not see her for many years.

The third sequence covers events from December 1926 to mid-1928. The first six chapters take Anthony through a party to which Mary has invited him unexpectedly, and at which he meets her daughter Helen. Mary's hedonistic and decadent life-style is taking its toll, and she is now reduced to having an affair with a down-at-heel aristocrat, who, as the sequence progresses, seduces Helen, who in turn marries another man on the rebound. We also see Anthony's old schoolfriend Mark Staithes who has become a communist in order to pursue an entirely self-centred nihilistic desire for revolution. In the fourth sequence, which consists of only two chapters dated May 1931, Helen has realised that her husband loves only a romanticised idea of her; meeting Anthony again, they begin a relationship.

The fifth sequence, from August 1933 to February 1934, opens the book with the famous chapter in which Helen and Anthony, their love having waned and their attachment only physical, are making love on the roof of their villa. In one of the bizarre, inexplicable and grotesque events with which Huxley was wont to symbolise the meaninglessness of life, they are interrupted when a dog, which has fallen out of an aeroplane, lands next to them and covers them both with blood. Both are deeply affected (who would not be?) by this event; Helen shuns Anthony entirely, but he for his part has realised that, although he has kept his emotional distance from her in order to preserve what he believes is his freedom, he has tender feelings for her which must now be forever unfulfilled. Both flirt with communism; Helen falls in love with Ekki, a German refugee, but when he is killed by the Nazis she realises that her political beliefs are hollow, and only her love for him was real. Anthony, meanwhile, accompanies Mark Staithes to Mexico to take part in a revolution. When Staithes is injured, they are fortunate to find the sage Miller (modelled on Dr MacPhail and F.M. Alexander), who treats him and who teaches Anthony something of the real meaning of existence.

The sixth sequence of chapters, which includes the final one, runs between April 1934 and February 1935, in which

Anthony's new life as a pacifist activist is described, via his diary and yet another meditation on Greville's 'Chorus Sacerdotum', as a movement from darkness/blindness to light. Mary Amberley, meanwhile, has finally descended into degradation and drug addiction. The novel ends with Anthony under threat of attack from fascist thugs at a speaking engagement, but he is tranquil about what might be in store for him: 'Whatever it might be, he knew now that all would be well.' Anthony's life has been largely a process of evasion of responsibility, driven by egotism and lack of empathy with others; at the end, partly inspired by the example of Ekki, he takes responsibility, and faces the uncertain future with courage.

The Olive Tree (1936)

The Olive Tree appeared on the cusp of Huxley's departure for the US, and feels like a tying up of loose ends. The title essay celebrated the Mediterranean culture which the Huxleys loved via a description of the contribution made by the cultivation of olives. 'D.H. Lawrence' was the introduction to Huxley's edition of the letters (1932), while 'T.H. Huxley as a Literary Man' was his T.H. Huxley lecture of the same year. Not all the pieces in *The Olive Tree* date from after the transformation of Huxley's political views; four pieces were taken from the mid-1920s. Yet at the time of publication, Huxley was unaware that he would never again be resident in Europe; it can hardly be assumed that he was consciously putting his literary affairs in order.

The new pieces began to flesh out Huxley's conversion in political terms. In 'Justifications', he argues that ideologies are merely post hoc rationalisations of basic desires. Propaganda, he claims in 'Writers and Readers', is most acceptable when it exhorts its readers to do what they otherwise wished to do. 'Words and Behaviour' looks at how military metaphor conceals the reality of bloodshed, and unpicks a contradiction at the heart of conditional pacifism, that the so-called pacifist must reserve the right to violence in the 'last resort' – but who can say when the last resort is upon us?

An Encyclopædia of Pacifism (1937)

It is not known how much of the *Encyclopædia of Pacifism* was written by Huxley; he was credited as editor, and no other contributor was mentioned. His published letters give no hint. Certainly some of the material ended up in his later book *Ends and Means*.

The *Encyclopædia* was much less grand than its title suggested: it is a small, pocket-sized pamphlet with, as its front cover boasted, 128 pages, fifty-five articles, price 6d (i.e. 2½p in modern British decimal currency, about £1.30 at 2011 prices). The articles were alphabetically arranged, from 'Armaments, Private Manufacture of' to 'Women in Modern War, Position of'. A number of uncompromising stances were taken. The article on 'Sanctions' argued that economic sanctions, applied with vigour, could only lead to war. 'Revolution' argued that no socialist could consistently take part in warfare: 'The people who will bear the brunt of the socialist airmen's attack will be workers and their wives and children.' The article on 'Propaganda' somewhat contradicted the thesis of *The Olive Tree*, by discussing the need for warmongers to inflame public opinion – hard to do if propaganda only justifies sentiments already held. 'The Peace Pledge Union' reiterated Huxley's previous call for an international conference to address grievances caused by the penal clauses in the Treaty of Versailles.

Ends and Means (1937)

As he left for America, Huxley suggested to his publisher that he was writing a 'philosophico-psychologico-sociological book' (a self-deprecatory phrase reminiscent of Dr Pangloss's discipline of metaphysico-theologico-cosmology in Voltaire's *Candide*). This book, although completed at Frieda Lawrence's ranch in New Mexico, was 'really' the final episode of Huxley's European/ pacifist period, where the rationale for mysticism was the pragmatic imperative of preventing war. At the time it was Huxley's most coherent full-length work of non-fiction, developing an argument that good ends can only be served by good means, and that therefore there was no such thing as a 'good' or 'just' war. The manner of the application or implementation of ideals matters as much as their content. Large-scale social reform could not be directed entirely at the alteration of social structures, but should also facilitate a change of heart for individuals; if it does not do both, then changing structures 'may deliver men from one set of evils, only to lead them to evils of another kind'. Human nature was not unchanging, and further transformation was necessary if a more peaceful society was to flourish. Violence could not effect that; instead, Huxley proposed decentralisation, education, the Alexander Technique and his old standbys of meditation and spiritual exercises.

Huxley's late ideas were gradually coming together, the tone more professorial, with fewer references to the poets and artists of the past, and many more to mystics, doctors, psychologists and sociologists. Nevertheless *Ends and Means* was not yet the authentic late Huxleian voice. Even if it is not as downright contradictory and confused as C.S. Ferns claims,[7] it is a pessimistic book with an optimistic message. Huxley, like many intellectuals of the time, was badly affected by the darkening war clouds, and (perhaps because his conversion was so recent) unable to adapt his pacifism to the new threatening world. He remained an unconditional pacifist, and could not find it within himself to sanction what he knew was inevitable, the war against Hitler (whom he despised). The result was a work that felt irrelevant, whose philosophy, however valid, had absolutely no chance of being adopted.

Thought

This period of Huxley's life contained his first major political activity, and a religious conversion, and unsurprisingly these changes in outlook were reflected in his work. His punishing self-portraits changed their character from this period onwards. The proxy-Huxley in *Eyeless in Gaza*, Anthony Beavis (like his later counterpart Sebastian Barnack in *Time Must Have a Stop*) is still ineffectual and remote, but unlike Gumbril or Philip Quarles he is going somewhere. It takes a while for him to come round to enlightenment, but by the end of the book enlightened he is. Similarly the prosy cynics like Scogan and Cardan evolved into the wise old sage Miller. The evidence of a step-change in Huxley's thought is clear from a comparison of *Eyeless in Gaza* with, say, *Antic Hay*.

Peace as a positive goal

The pursuit of an intellectual rationale for pacifism led to his exploration of mystical religion. One attraction of mysticism for Huxley was that it could provide an account of the wearisome condition that could satisfy him rationally. In a 1935 review of a translation of Pareto's *The Mind and Society*, he argued that the search for rationality was as important to the human as hunger and thirst. Rationality he specifically defined as 'unification of diversity', and pointed out that though we often have to make do with more complex schemes such as 'the Ten Commandments, the Nine Beatitudes, the Eightfold Way, the hunger and thirst after rationality can never be fully assuaged except by the One'. As often with Huxley, he was attracted to an idea that he had originally explored ironically, and much of his future career was spent trying to find ways of expressing the unity and diversity of existence simultaneously.

But the possibility of unification of diversity was not his most pressing concern. At this stage, the politics came first.

Huxley wanted peace. Mysticism was a precondition for peace, and so peace implied mysticism and love. Though this seemed very straightforward (see the entries from Anthony Beavis's notebook in *Eyeless in Gaza*), it was not practical politics. Huxley's pamphlet *What Are You Going To Do About It?* was undermined by the inevitable critical focus on its positive communitarian ideal; the meditation and spiritual exercises were not only odd, but also the sort of faddish silliness that Huxley the ironist used to lampoon. However, it is important to separate out the first eleven sections of the pamphlet, in which Huxley set out the logical case for unconditional pacifism, from the final one with the supposedly practical implementation strategy. Huxley's use of Darwinism, and of human history, showed that war is neither inevitable nor desirable, while his dissection of political and religious arguments in favour of war was forensic. His faith in experts and his lack of understanding of realpolitik emerged in his plea for a conference – one does wonder where Huxley's perpetual hope in conferences came from, especially as he attended and complained about so many during his life.

The pursuit of peace, as in any other moral endeavour, would be undermined if inconsistent means were used to produce the desired ends; hence one could secure peace neither by war nor by the threat of war. He argued that the net result of liberal humanism, the civilised philosophy of the Bloomsbury intellectuals, was nationalism, which implied conflict and ultimately warfare, and concluded that the best metaphysical foundation for pacifism was a spiritual reality over and above our this-worldly surroundings. It seems that, at least originally, this mystical reality was premised on the imperative to find a ground for pacifism, not the other way around. The need to organise our world so that arbitrary killing did not take place required an alternative reality which could liberate people from earthly concerns.

Whether or not one is convinced by them, sections I–XI of *What Are You Going To Do About It?* demand to be taken seriously.

Pacifism was popular in the interwar democracies. Why, then, did Huxley risk losing his audience with the final positive manifesto of spiritual exercises and meditation? There are three reasons, which we explore in the next three sections: the need to weld a group of disparate individuals into an effective political unit; the need to combat opposing ideologies; and the inability of tools such as science, technology and education to create a good society.

The role of the individual

Huxley's diagnosis of the peace campaigners' problem was more accurate than most in the anti-war camp in the 1930s. Interwar pacifism has a curious modern parallel with environmentalism. Many if not most people believe that human actions are threatening the planet, and yet agreeing concerted action is proving almost completely impossible; the same was true, analogously, in the 1930s when most people opposed war and yet the common consensus was that war was clearly coming. Huxley realised that fragmentation of the anti-war opinion was a handicap; some pacifists were communists, some religious, some were powerfully committed, others less so, some believed that might was right in the face of an aggressive fascist warmonger, while others thought peace should be unconditional. The anti-war camp totalled several millions of British people at its peak who disagreed about (a) how to pursue peace, (b) when to stop pursuing peace, and (c) how important peace was. Some were prepared to make enormous personal sacrifices, some were prepared to invest time and resources, while most were willing only to make positive noises from the sidelines. More people needed to make an effort, and their efforts needed to be coordinated and targeted.

Huxley realised that a diverse set of people would struggle to achieve power, and argued that if pacifism were to become an effective political ideology, it would need to cohere around a group of like-minded people, as had socialism, conservatism and many types of nationalism. Those ideologies provided unifying myths to focus the efforts of their adherents.

Yet this was surely not a coherent position for the author of *Brave New World*. In the first place, Huxley must have known that the spiritual exercises of the type he prescribed might work for small communities of inner-directed people, but there was no evidence that it could drive the pan-European movement that he had in mind. Fascism and Nazism brought together large numbers of people with the use of crude symbolism, but Huxley had no truck with that kind of rabble-rousing based on the demonization of minorities. He did argue that a single pacifist nation could act as an important example to others, and – even if in hindsight we know that the courses of Hitler's Germany and Mussolini's Italy were well set by 1936 – it is just possible (although few believe it) that a clear renunciation of war by Baldwin or Chamberlain towards the end of the 1930s would have produced a happier outcome than did the difficult balance they tried to strike between appeasement of German territorial ambitions and surreptitious rearmament in the background. Even so, Huxley's decentralised communities would have had to produce a pacifist breakthrough in at least one significant nation and he had no reason to think that that was on the cards at any stage.

Second, and perhaps more damaging for Huxley's reputation as a consistent thinker is the reflection that *Brave New World* is all about the inauthentic formation of preferences. Bad things happen not because they are imposed on people, but because they are conditioned to *want* the bad things. Inauthenticity is an evil when people are hoodwinked into misunderstanding their own interests. Yet wasn't Huxley trying to develop social structures to promote a particular outcome that people may not have been comfortable with? Granted Huxley was more benign than Mustapha Mond – even so, wasn't his aim to design a society that *caused* people to think and act politically in pre-determined ways?

Science and technology as means to ends: eugenics revisited

Huxley's admiration for science, technology, social science and management was tempered by the realisation that they were two-edged weapons, which could be used for evil. But whereas many thinkers now would argue that the use of technology to steer people in particular directions is wrong per se, Huxley argues in *Ends and Means* that it is only wrong to steer people in the wrong direction; setting them in the right direction is a good use of technology. Huxley began to insist more frequently and power-fully that science and technology were tools that could be used for good or evil. He denied the possibility of unalloyed progress through science, but equally was alive to the improvements that could be made to lives and knowledge if only science was used wisely. So science could not improve people, before people had already been improved.

Yet the argument of *Ends and Means* that good ends can only be reached using good means doesn't really square with that idea. If we wish to be good, and if science is morally neutral, then how can we determine which scientific or technological means are good and which bad? What counts morally in the application of science are precisely the ends to which it is put. One is forced, as a scientist, to examine the ends – and quite often of course the applied scientist is in ignorance of how a piece of science will be used. The distinction between good means and bad means cannot simply be read off the distinction between good and bad ends, even if the latter distinction is a simple one.

Which it is not. Let us take an example. As the depression began to bite, Huxley rekindled his interest in eugenics, and his conclusions in essays written in the 1930s became much less equivocal than in his 'Note on Eugenics' from *Proper Studies*. In a piece from 1934,[8] he advocated compulsory sterilisation 'on humanitarian grounds', of 'idiots', 'imbeciles' and 'the feeble-minded' (Huxley estimated that there were 200,000 feeble-minded people 'at large'). Although he trusted the experts of the 'Mental Deficiency Committee' (County and County Borough Council institutions mandatory under the 1913 Mental Deficiency Act) and the Eugenics Society, he also rather inconsistently demanded 'a minimum of vexatious State interference'. He often made the assumption that future governments would need some kind of eugenic policy.

The distinction between 'good' eugenics, and 'bad' social engineering *Brave New World*-style, is not always obvious. Perhaps the most plausible reconstruction of Huxley's ideas is that 'good' eugenics assumes a decent quality of life, and winnows out all those unable to enjoy such a life, or whose existence puts the quality of life of everyone else at risk, while 'bad' social engineering tries to create human beings suited to dehumanising mass production and mass consumption. This is probably not a distinction that a modern reader will find convincing.

However that may be, he dismissed the objections of 'mystical democrats' that eugenics was unwarranted social engineering as unscientific. Yet surely to reject a moral argument on scientific grounds is to put the scientific cart before the moral horse – which the whole argument of *Ends and Means* denies is legitimate.

Huxley's main focus was on the questions of peace, war and pacifism of the 1930s. Is it acceptable to kill, or declare war, in order to prevent more killing or to stop Hitler? These are not simple questions to answer – had they been, the peace movement would not have fragmented and collapsed.

Ideology and irrationality

Huxley's original opposition to absolutist political and religious thinking was premised on a reading of Pareto (the history sections of *Brave New World* leaned on Pareto heavily, and he wrote a number of essays in the mid-1930s exploring Pareto's hierarchical views and disbelief in progress). The major cultural clashes of the twentieth century, claimed Huxley, could be explained by Pareto's theory of actions and preferences which, though rationalised by the actors, are driven by emotion and irrationality. One such type of preference was the tendency of people to tolerate diversity, enabling them to combine ideas or actions in order to achieve goals, or alternatively through the sheer love of experiment. This could be contrasted with a second (conservative) tendency of people to defend established aggregates and to resist their disintegration, if necessary by fighting to the death.

Huxley, who loved social classification schemes, used this idea to explain, for instance, the Nazi revolution: the tolerant Weimar Republicans (combiners) were too tolerant to prevent the fascists (resisters) slaughtering them in a bloody struggle. In twentieth-century societies, people in whom the instinct for combination was strong tended to rise up the social scale (because their ideas added more value economically and socially), while those who supported the persistence of aggregates tended to be lower down the hierarchy. Where people of the first type predominated, the result was an over-rational, tolerant polity (like Weimar) which would not seek to prevent dangerous fundamentalists from thriving and ultimately overthrowing the regime. Where people of the second type predominated, the result was conservatism and war. The ideal, for Huxley in the mid-1930s at least, was a society where the people of the second type were in charge, but where their politicians, scientists and financiers were of the first type, so society was protected and social creativity was retained where it mattered.

As time moved on, so did Huxley move on from Pareto, and he began to develop his own ideas. In 'Justifications' from *The Olive Tree*, he examined the role of abstract thought and philosophy in fomenting and provoking conflict where otherwise there would be none:

> Unsophisticated by thought, anger soon dies down; but supply a
> man with a philosophy proving that he is right to be angry, and

he will go on performing in cold blood the acts of malice which otherwise he could have performed only when the fit was upon him.

Two religions, for example, may agree on many things including the existence and goodness of God, but their respective theologians, grasping vainly for the truth, formulate key dogmata differently ('God is three persons'/'God is one person'). These statements are pretty meaningless, and are really trying to deploy the inadequate resources of language to describe some ineffable truth. The statements no doubt have roles to play within the ritual of the churches, but they don't advance our understanding significantly. Yet for the adherents of the two churches they become key signifiers of the ideas that unite them; they express group identities. Within each church, the contrary metaphysical statement comes to seem like a deliberate insult, a negation of all it holds dear. Each church becomes the embodiment of evil for the other. And now, thanks to the fatal combination of linguistic inadequacy and group dynamics, we have the raw materials for religious persecution and war. In each group, the shibboleths of the other come to be seen as impugning its identity, and therefore as an attack on its God. Mere death is not good enough for its members. Torture and the Inquisition are called for.

Huxley was fascinated by the religious cruelty of the seventeenth century, and powerfully drew out its parallels with the mid-twentieth century. Ideologues had got rid of their metaphysical baggage, but they still reduced reality to simple morally tinged fables with far-reaching consequences. He realised that absolutist abstraction was not restricted to the religious sphere, although it would always give rise to a quasi-religious faith in whatever secular 'ism' a zealot had chosen, whether communism, fascism or nationalism. Nationalism in particular offended him; in *Beyond the Mexique Bay* his tour of many Latin American nations led him to complain that its chief products were war and red tape. The problem was not only governments; the individual had a responsibility too. In *Eyeless in Gaza*, one character argues that patriotism 'fulfils our worst wishes. In the person of our nation we are able, vicariously, to bully and cheat.'

On Huxley's account, nations were ultimately groups of individuals who could not escape responsibility for the nation's actions, and whose attitudes were the fundamental explanation for its deeds. Here he echoed Proust, who had written in *Time Regained* that the life of a nation:

> merely repeats, on a larger scale, the lives of its component cells: and he who is incapable of understanding the mystery, the reactions, the laws that determine the movements of the individual, can never hope to say anything worth listening to about the struggles of Peoples.

Hence the roots of malevolent political power could be found in individuals' own hatred of others.

As Huxley wrote in *Ends and Means*, 'there must be more than a mere deflection of evil; there must be suppression at the source, in the individual will'. This, no less, was the task of the political leader. It was easy to harness ill-feeling with rabble-rousing oratory, but somehow – whether by the spiritual exercises or otherwise – choices must be changed at the level of the individual. This is the second reason why he believed that the decentralised communities by which he set such store would need to cohere around some tangible set of ideas and/or traditions and practices. He hoped these could be provided artificially, basing his hopes on the psychological literature which showed greater levels of happiness and socialisation among religious people.

There is no doubt that Huxley's contemporary analysis of the motivations and politics of the mid-century ideologues, hugely controversial at the time, especially among fellow travellers who implicitly favoured one side, is broadly shared by most historians.

For instance, Timothy Snyder has recently written that both Hitler and Stalin 'had a transformative Utopia, a group to be blamed when its realisation proved impossible, and then a policy of mass murder that could be proclaimed as a kind of ersatz victory'.[9] This corresponds exactly to Huxley's diagnosis.

Educating against ideology

How could the hold of words over minds be broken? As ever with Huxley, educational solutions were not far from his thoughts, but at this time he was not at all optimistic. Ten years after his previous major pronouncement on education in *Proper Studies*, Huxley returned to the topic with a long chapter towards the end of *Ends and Means*. Surprisingly, given his earlier enthusiasms, neither the Dalton Plan nor Miss Parkhurst is mentioned, and indeed some of his claims are completely at odds with the philosophy of individualised learning. Now, he argued that 'There is a danger that children may be given more freedom than they can profitably deal with, more responsibility than they desire or know how to take.'

This may have had something to do with perceived problems in Matthew's enrolment at the experimental Dartington Hall about this time. Dartington's philosophy was to give the child a lot of autonomy, and Matthew had chosen to concentrate on carpentry, much to his parents' chagrin. They had assumed, quite without debate, that he should be a doctor; Aldous had much more traditional views of education as a parent than he did as a theorist. In the end, the Huxleys whisked Matthew away from Dartington without any warning at the end of one term, and put him in the Institut Rauch in Lausanne. By the time *Ends and Means* was being written, the family was en route to the US.

By 1937, Huxley felt that positive change in one sector of society could not happen in isolation; society had to change all at once and all together, not piecemeal. It followed from this that Huxley did not hold out much hope for free and universal education; even if such an education was good (and he did not expect it to be), its recipients would still have to live in our unsatisfactory world:

> When we compare the high hopes entertained by the early advocates of universal education with the results actually achieved after two generations of intensive and extensive teaching, we cannot fail to be somewhat discouraged. Millions of children have passed thousands of millions of hours under schoolroom discipline, reading the Bible, listening to pi-jaws [i.e. tedious moral lectures] – and the peoples of the world are preparing for mutual slaughter more busily and more scientifically than ever before; humanitarianism is visibly declining; the idolatrous worship of strong men is on the increase; international politics are conducted with a degree of brutal cynicism unknown since the days of Pope Alexander VI and Cesare Borgia.

He cited Maria Montessori and Bertrand Russell to demonstrate the link between the new militarism and harsh school discipline: 'The traditional education is a training for life in a hierarchical, militaristic society, in which people are abjectly obedient to their superiors and inhuman to their inferiors.' Although he was critical of the democracies, he explicitly argued that their systems were superior to those of the fascist and communist states. Education as traditionally conceived, like science, was inadequate by itself to create a good, peaceful, tolerant society. People had to change before education could be a benefit.

As Milton Birnbaum has argued,[10] Huxley probably only had a tenuous grasp on what an education was actually like in England or America for most children – Matthew's was hardly average. His main argument by the time *Ends and Means* appeared was that children should be taught critical thinking and scepticism. Language in particular should be scrutinised for misleading metaphors and abstractions. The child – and here Huxley was actually making no real distinction between children and adults – should be taught to resist suggestion.

6
Mystic, 1937–53

Life

On board the *Normandie*, the Huxleys had the royal treatment –
having paid for tourist class they were upgraded to a luxurious
cabin and given the freedom of the ship. Ironically, their neighbour from Sanary, Thomas Mann, already a Nobel laureate, was
kept in tourist. The fêting continued in New York, where the
Huxleys were overwhelmed with how in demand Aldous
now was for interviews and radio. They bought a Ford and
Maria drove the party to Frieda Lawrence's ranch near Taos,
New Mexico, via various universities and medical institutions, in
five weeks (Christopher Wood went on ahead separately to
Hollywood). The effort of driving in rough terrain was a severe
effort for the slightly built Maria, who was down to ninety-eight
pounds upon arrival.

Frieda was one of the twentieth century's great eccentrics.
A relative of the flying ace Baron von Richthofen, she had married a philologist at Nottingham University before eloping with
his former student Lawrence. After his death, she returned to
their ranch where the Huxleys found her ensconced with an
Italian lover, and Dorothy Brett; Brett and Frieda were not on
speaking terms, as the former had tried to steal Lawrence's ashes
from their chapel of rest in order to sprinkle them over the ranch.

Huxley fell in love with the desert, though Maria was unsure,
homesick and appalled at the lack of servants. Matthew preferred
Hollywood. Aldous completed *Ends and Means*, which sold
extremely well as a worked-out philosophy of unconditional
pacifism. Surprisingly, given his low opinion of the talkies, Huxley

was intrigued when approached by Los Angeles bookseller Jake Zeitlin who offered to introduce him to the movie industry. Maria liked the sound of the money that could be made, but Huxley's first effort, *Success*, a satirical comedy based on the power of advertising, attracted interest but no takers.

Completion of *Ends and Means* was followed by a lecture tour about peace and pacifism, initially with Heard and Huxley doing a double act ('Mutt and Jeff', as Huxley described the pairing). After Heard broke his shoulder Huxley soldiered on, alone and unwilling, although there was the bonus in Chicago, of meeting Dr William Sheldon, a psychologist whose classification of human body types was to be a strong influence. Poor Maria was exhausted by the driving. In September they found a flat in Hollywood and joined the intellectual society that had gathered in the home of the movies; the power of that industry began to dawn on Huxley who had been so stuffy about *The Jazz Singer* a decade before. As well as reacquainting themselves with Anita Loos and Charlie Chaplin and his then-partner Paulette Goddard, they met several celebrities, and formed a new social circle including the astronomer Edwin Hubble and his wife Grace, Harpo Marx, the writer Christopher Isherwood and composer Igor Stravinsky. There is some dispute as to whether Maria took part in what would have been scandalous gatherings of Hollywood's underground network of lesbian contacts known as 'sewing circles'.[1]

In 1938 they took up permanent residence in Los Angeles, though remained peripatetic – they had notched up three different Hollywood addresses by the end of the year. After Huxley had shaken off a bronchial condition he began work first on a novel that was never finished, and then on the piece that became *After Many a Summer*, while continuing his psycho-sociological studies expressly for the purpose of 'giving a viable economic and social basis to philosophical anarchism'. If Huxley had not changed his *mind* about the importance of the open-minded pursuit of knowledge, he had certainly changed his *practice*; his studies were now intended to confirm and bolster a particular theory, rather than to explore the world without prejudice.

Huxley's screenwriting career gained momentum. He was paid $15,000 for a biopic of Marie Curie, although his contribution was not used. His first credited script, for *Pride and Prejudice*, directed by Robert Z. Leonard for MGM and starring Laurence Olivier and Greer Garson, was written in late 1939. Huxley reportedly found directors and stars frustrating, but was pleased with the resulting film (which won an Oscar for art direction). *Jane Eyre*, directed by Robert Stevenson, with Orson Welles and Joan Fontaine for Twentieth Century Fox followed. The large fees that Huxley earned from the cinema enabled him to help the Nys family, once again impoverished as their home was over-run by German invaders for the second time; the Huxleys sent food and other goods to Belgium, and between 1939 and 1944 extended their hospitality to Maria's niece Sophie Neveux when she escaped Europe. Ironically, Huxley had made good at the very moment that his literary agents were exposed as fraudsters. He was swindled out of over £500, a sum he would have felt keenly even a couple of years previously.

In late 1939, Huxley's first American novel appeared, *After Many a Summer*, in which he indulged his taste for grotesquerie, and poked fun both at America's glitzy and beguiling oddness, and the England he was leaving behind. In any event, the book was better received in America than England. The next project, suggested to him by Gerald Heard in 1940, was a biography of Richelieu's confidant and agent Père Joseph; research and writing went well, although getting hold of the necessary books from Europe was problematic, and the book appeared as *Grey Eminence* in 1941.

Under Heard's influence, Huxley was getting interested in Eastern philosophy, and it was about this time that he met J. Krishnamurti, who had been adopted by Annie Besant and the theosophists at the age of fourteen and groomed to be a world

teacher of spiritual truth. Now, thirty years later, he had settled in
California where he had developed a philosophy not unlike
Huxley's, that revolution must be fostered in people's psyches,
and could not be imposed by outside political entities. Huxley
and Heard also attended meetings of the Vedanta Society of
Southern California, run by the Swami Prabhavananda. A third
influence was Eileen Garrett, a medium to whom the Huxleys
were introduced in 1941. Huxley also kept a weather eye on
Heard's experiments in community-based living.

Huxley's interest in alternative medical therapies brought him
to the Bates Method of exercising the eyes; on one uncorrobor-
ated account, his doctors had warned him in 1939 that he was
approaching blindness.[2] Under the Bates regimen, his sight
(which had already responded very well to the Californian light)
improved dramatically, prompting him to pen a small volume
extolling its virtues. *The Art of Seeing* is primarily a self-help book,
but remains of interest as light and its absence often played
important symbolic roles in Huxley's works. He was able to write
and revise *After Many a Summer* without recourse to spectacles,
and indeed eschewed optical aids for many years. In one of her
letters of the 1940s, Maria notes that Aldous's publicity photo-
graphs were now very rarely retouched to make his eyes look
'normal'.

Maria had grown to love the desert, and the Huxleys moved
outside Los Angeles when the film work died down at the end of
1941. They moved to a small retreat, Llano del Rio, a forty-acre
site in the Mojave Desert about fifty miles away. Aldous continued to suffer with his health, particularly after he strained his
heart doing heavy labour, but Maria, who had been having respi-
ratory problems, improved in the clear desert air. She enjoyed
Llano's austere beauty, but Aldous did no housework, so she
ended up as the skivvy, as she reminded most of her correspondents. Matthew spent some time there during leave from the
US Army Medical Corps, while Maria's youngest sister Rose,

together with toddler and baby, joined them in 1943. Aldous spent time in Los Angeles working at the studios, and also at Heard's community at Trabuco, and completed a new novel, *Time Must Have a Stop*, in 1943, before moving on to work on an anthology with commentary of statements of and about mystical philosophy and experience.

This latter work, *The Perennial Philosophy*, provided the reader with an access point to what Huxley called the 'Highest Common Factor' underlying the great religions of the world, which he believed could act as a foundation for post-war reconstruction. He was disillusioned with the prospects for post-war society, and pessimistic about the ultimate effects of the War. His fear that reconstruction would generate a centralised, interfering bureaucracy echoed political philosopher Friedrich Hayek's *The Road to Serfdom*, written about this time. Huxley eschewed Hayek's free market theories, preferring a peaceful, decentralised world order underpinned by a shared outlook across and between cultures. He hoped that his description of the perennial philosophy would make it obvious that most major metaphysical systems were founded around a strong common core which could act as the basis for such an outlook.

In the end, the ranch at Llano proved impossible – the housework proved too much for Maria while Aldous developed an allergy to some of the desert fauna, and the Huxleys (still shuttling in and out of Los Angeles) moved to a mountain retreat at Wrightwood in 1946, Matthew and his girlfriend eventually joining them and living together at a second house on the property. At this stage, Matthew, now in his mid-twenties, was working for Warner Brothers as a reader, and was also prominent in union activities; he had campaigned for Roosevelt in the 1944 election, and had also helped lead a strike, persuading his father to join him in both activities.

Huxley was preoccupied for some time in the mid-1940s with a historical novel about St Catherine of Siena, fourteenth-century patron saint of Italy who had had mystical experiences from childhood, and had experienced a 'mystical marriage' with Christ. Huxley saw contemporary relevance in her selfless work for peace between Italy's warring republics that resulted in her death from exhaustion and malnutrition at the age of thirty-three. That novel never reached fruition; instead 1946 saw the publication of a small tract called *Science, Liberty and Peace*, and he began work for Universal on a film version (with an altered ending) of his story 'The Giaconda Smile' from the *Mortal Coils* collection, which eventually saw the light of day as *A Woman's Vengeance* directed by Zoltan Korda and starring Charles Boyer. His next novel, *Ape and Essence*, a fierce fantasy, appeared in 1948, to poor reviews. Nevertheless, Huxley was confident in his approach; reality was outdoing fiction in absurdity.

In September 1947, they drove to New York – amazingly for such a peripatetic couple, this was the first time they had left California for nearly ten years – and in 1948 returned to Europe, seeing family and old friends and acquaintances, and researching the St Catherine book. Some time was spent at Sanary, where Maria's sister Jeanne had stored their possessions. Among the books Huxley found there was his edition of the obscure nineteenth-century philosopher Maine de Biran's *Journal Intime*, which he had first read and copiously annotated in 1931; he now embarked on a serious historical-biographical-philosophical study in the style of *Grey Eminence*.

Back in the US, Huxley's health took several turns for the worse. He was plagued with bronchial illnesses, while his eyes were weakened by an attack of flu; for several months in 1951 he lost all sight in his weaker right eye. The illnesses were accompanied by new fads, including parapsychology, séances, hypnosis, auto-hypnosis, attempts to reach their deeper selves, unidentified flying objects (a particular interest of Heard's) and L. Ron Hubbard's dianetics. The Huxleys fell in love with a new house in Los Angeles, and spent the next few months completing the

Maine de Biran piece, which, although twice as long as some of his books, was published as part of the essay collection *Themes and Variations*. It was about this time that Huxley corresponded with George Orwell, who had sent him a copy of *Nineteen Eighty-Four*. Huxley responded politely to Orwell's overture but argued that his own dystopia *Brave New World* captured the complex strategy of controlling preferences that would characterise late twentieth-century government, while the brute force and repression that Orwell envisaged was a less practical and realistic route to totalitarianism. For his own part, Orwell throughout his career was dismissive of Huxley's work.

The year 1950 brought the Huxleys back to Europe, via New York where they attended Matthew's wedding (they became grandparents to Mark Trevenen Huxley in October 1951), to do more research on St Catherine. Huxley's oft-repeated remark that the world's political travails could only be a case of widespread demoniacal possession, translated itself into a new idea. He would write the story of the diabolic events at Loudun in 1634 when a group of nuns was found to be possessed en masse by the devil, resulting in a series of vile tortures and executions. The seventeenth century was his favourite historical period, and he realised that the narrative could be used as a prop for his own gloomy analysis of the analogous state of the modern world. *The Devils of Loudun*, one of Huxley's masterpieces, was published in 1952; once more many critics were repelled by the violence, torture and pessimism.

Earlier that year, Maria had fallen ill with a cyst on her breast which turned out to be malignant. The prognosis was bad; a mastectomy was performed. She found many of the Californian mystical practices a comfort, quit her vegetarianism and shared her worries with her friends in letters. It is not known whether Aldous was, at this stage, aware of quite how ill she was; they spent much of their time simply enjoying life together, holidaying in the Arizona desert. Certainly many of their friends remarked at this time on their serenity.

Work

After Many a Summer/After Many a Summer Dies the Swan (1939)

The first of Huxley's works written entirely in America was finished the day before his forty-fifth birthday. *After Many a Summer* was the most plot-driven of his novels up to that point. It took its title from a line from 'Tithonus', Tennyson's poem about the mythical Trojan prince loved by a water nymph, who gives him the gift of immortality. But because she forgets to give him eternal youth, he eventually becomes a wretched, gibbering old man.

After Many a Summer (the American title quoted the whole of the relevant line) is about ageing and the Californian cult of eternal youth. Jo Stoyte is a W.R. Hearst-like millionaire living in a fake castle full of a hoard of great art works (there are close similarities to Orson Welles's film *Citizen Kane*, which *After Many a Summer* preceded by a couple of years). Stoyte employs Jeremy Pordage, an English scholar, to catalogue his collection of rare books; through Pordage's bewildered eyes we are introduced to America as a land of incredible, baffling contrasts. Also in Stoyte's employ is the scientist Dr Obispo, who has been hired to find ways of extending Stoyte's life; the business-hardened Stoyte is terrified by the thought of death. Obispo is a charming villain, entirely self-centred, wholly evil, destructive of illusion, who seduces Stoyte's mistress Virginia, and uses his hold over Stoyte to persuade him to turn a blind eye. When Jeremy discovers a reference in an old text suggesting that immortality has been achieved by an eighteenth-century English aristocrat, Obispo and Stoyte see their opportunity. The full cost of attachment to life is revealed in the twist ending.

The one positive character in the book is Stoyte's neighbour Mr Propter, loosely based on Heard. Blessed with equivalent vision and insight to Obispo, he is morally committed to enabling and encouraging people to welcome a spiritual dimension into their lives, to make sense of the confusing world in which they live. He offers freedom from illusion, whereas Obispo uses the illusions of those he corrupts, like a modern-day scientific, capitalistic, rationalistic Mephistopheles. Sadly, Propter, like Miller in *Eyeless in Gaza*, is something of a bore, and his ideas waffly and half-formed.

After Many a Summer is undeniably minor, but an enjoyably rollicking fantasy nonetheless. What strikes the reader, particularly after *Eyeless in Gaza*, is a new exuberance. The commentaries of Propter, however tedious, add a certain depth, preventing the novel from being an entirely negative and ironic take on modern consumerist life, and the inability of modern man to accept with grace the accidents of fate. Pordage's early experiences of Los Angeles, mirroring Huxley's own astonishment, communicate great pleasure at the meaningless pastiche; Stoyte's castle 'was Gothic, mediaeval, baronial – doubly baronial, Gothic with Gothicity raised, so to speak, to a higher power, more mediaeval than any building of the thirteenth century'.

Grey Eminence (1941)

In *Grey Eminence*, Huxley explored a genre new to him, reporting history with a novelist's pen. He used his narrative skills to dramatise the differences and similarities between his chosen period and the present, showing how feelings about religion had changed the way people reacted to events, and how, by implication, functionally similar constructs (such as ideology and consumerism) had taken religion's place in the modern world. His novelistic sketches made characters memorable in ways that dry academic lists of the scanty records would make difficult. Strict accuracy was sacrificed – for example, Huxley tended to report rumour as fact if it fitted his narrative. But that didn't really matter, as the main purpose was to illustrate important themes of his own politics.

Three times he used this quasi-fictional genre, all in French settings: in *Grey Eminence*, 'Variations on a Philosopher', and finally *The Devils of Loudun*.

Grey Eminence illustrates the thesis of *Ends and Means* that good ends cannot be served by evil means, using the career of Père Joseph, a Capuchin friar in the service of Cardinal Richelieu, Louis XIII's first minister, in early seventeenth-century France. A minor nobleman attached to the French court, Joseph was influenced by the English contemplative mystic and heretic Benet of Canfield, whose *Way of Perfection* Huxley admired. Joseph followed Benet into the Capuchin order, and became a mystic himself, practising meditation and experiencing ecstatic joys.

His work in church administration brought Joseph into contact with Richelieu, who wielded a network of spies to curb the powers of the French nobles and centralise political control in the person of the king (and, not coincidentally, ministers such as himself). Joseph became his willing agent (he was the person for whom the descriptive term '*éminence grise*' was coined), leading a systematic campaign of subversion and corruption to break the power of the Protestant Huguenots within France.

Huxley dramatises the 'religious psychology' of Joseph, who rationalised his mean and amoral actions as an attempt to disseminate the true version of Christianity throughout the world. France was God's chosen instrument, and so the aggrandisement of France was essential, whatever means were used. The result was the prolongation of the Thirty Years' War (1618–48), one of the bloodiest episodes of religious violence in European history, devastating Germany, where it was largely fought, and impoverishing the people of France, whose taxes had to pay for the French involvement. Père Joseph, a saintly man in many ways, died an object of hatred.

Huxley wrote *Grey Eminence* as a tragedy, to illustrate his doctrine of evil means. In this, it succeeds brilliantly. It also includes his first real attempt to produce a systematic mystical philosophy, but that task would be superseded by *The Perennial Philosophy*.

The Art of Seeing (1942)

One of the oddest pieces of Huxley's varied output was *The Art of Seeing*, a self-help book based on the Bates Method for improving vision. The bulk of the book is a series of exercises for the mind and the eyes, but for the Huxley scholar the interest really lies in the opening section where the philosophy of the Bates Method is introduced. Huxley was by now convinced of the close connections between body and mind. Although this was not then an unusual position, it ran against the mainstream philosophy of Cartesian dualism, which postulated a complete conceptual rift between ethereal, extensionless mind and the extended physical body. Huxley developed the unified mind/body picture more clearly than most professional philosophers by focusing on the important effects of quotidian bodily processes, functions and ailments. Chronic pain, for instance, or a weak constitution will have a strong effect on the mental outlook. These 'minor' issues tend to be ignored by philosophers concerned with major psychological principles; Huxley with his novelist's eye saw how they would impinge powerfully on felt experience of daily life.

Huxley now argued that seeing was a psychological process involving mind and body working together. He borrowed C.D. Broad's account of perception as an amalgam of *sensing* the outside world using the eye, and gaining uninterpreted information about light and colour levels, *selecting* the phenomena of interest based on various heuristics (e.g. changes of light levels, indications of movement), and *perceiving* the world, that is, interpreting the sense data as objects.[3] Huxley objected to the use of artificial lenses to correct defective vision, as that only addressed the first of these processes and neglected the other two. Other organs or limbs when injured or disabled are trained to redevelop and regain former strength and skills using methods such as physio-therapy; the eye is treated differently. Its disablement is taken as read, merely compensated for; there is no attempt to improve the injured or diseased eye.

The Bates Method, which Huxley claimed had improved his vision, instead takes the entire psychological process of vision as a unified whole, and tries to improve perception by a variety of methods, which include not only physical exercises to improve the muscles controlling the eye, but also changing the posture, relaxing as one pays attention to something, or providing optimal lighting conditions. Huxley was clearly an enthusiast; it is fair to say that within the ophthalmology profession the reaction both to Bates's work and to Huxley's book was deeply sceptical. To date, there is no empirical evidence that the Bates Method improves eyesight.

Time Must Have a Stop (1944)

Huxley's second American novel reminds one of his early novellas with its settings in Italy and among the high English bourgeoisie. The title is once more Shakespearean, Hotspur's last words in *Henry IV Part I*:

> But thought's the slave of life, and life time's fool;
> And time, that takes survey of all the world,
> Must have a stop.

In 1959, Huxley expanded on his regard for this 'extraordinary phrase':

> It is one of those fantastic things one finds in Shakespeare; in a line and a half he throws out an entire philosophy and then passes on to something else. 'Thought's the slave of life', we

cannot think abstractly without being involved as physiological beings, as members of this living community on the planet; and 'life time's fool', the passing of time tends to undermine everything and produce constant change; and yet 'time, that takes survey of all the world, must have a stop', there is a religious, spiritual side to life – time must have a stop in the timeless and eternal world. It is these three worlds – the world of abstractions and concepts, the world of immediate experience and objective observation, and the world of spiritual insight – which must, in any integrated point of view, be brought together.[4]

The bulk of the novel is set in 1929, and concerns the beautiful, precocious, selfish young poet Sebastian Barnack, whose father is an idealistic socialist bore, and whose Uncle Eustace is a gluttonous bon viveur. Sebastian, wishing to enter into high society, is desperate for evening clothes which his puritanical father refuses to buy him. Salvation appears to be at hand on a visit to his uncle in Florence, when Eustace not only promises to buy him the suit, but also gives him a Degas drawing. Sebastian is overjoyed, but no sooner have the gifts been promised than Eustace expires on a visit to the lavatory.

Sebastian sells the drawing and buys himself the evening clothes, but when an inventory is made of Eustace's household contents, the Degas is reported missing; and an innocent child accused of theft. Sebastian, lacking proof of ownership, is too cowardly to admit what he has done, so he prevails upon an old Christian friend of Eustace, Bruno Rontini, to get the drawing back. It is returned and the *imbroglio* resolved, but as a result of a careless remark by Sebastian, Rontini is arrested by the fascists. Sebastian is initially remorseful, but forgets his betrayal and carries on his selfish life.

Thus far, the story is a regular Huxleian sardonic tale, not unlike 'Little Archimedes' or 'After the Fireworks'. Yet two sets of passages distinguish it from these. First of all, the death and immediate afterlife of Eustace is told as a stream of consciousness in which the old sybarite battles against a pure, beautiful light which draws him to sublimate and annihilate his old self. Yet he cannot divest himself of his earthly existence even for the promise of eternal bliss, remaining drawn to the beauties that sustained him through life; in the end he is reborn as the son of the art dealer who betrayed Rontini. This piece of experimental writing is remarkably extended, featuring in seven chapters; the effect is impressive, though maybe the sequences would have benefited from a little less of Huxley's trademark clarity and a little more inspired surrealism.

Second, the tale has an Epilogue of some thirty-six pages which takes us to the present day (1944), when Sebastian is now thirty-two. We learn of his selfish adulthood; he betrayed his wife at the point of her death with Veronica Thwale, who had many years earlier taken Sebastian's virginity. A chance encounter with the dying Rontini allowed the charitable old bookseller to show Sebastian how to live and die correctly, to live in the eternal world as well as in time. Extensive extracts from Sebastian's journal give examples of Rontini's philosophy; Rontini himself is more likeable than wordier sages such as Miller and Propter. The journal itself gives a first glimpse of what Huxley called the 'Minimum Working Hypothesis', that there is a transcendent, immanent Godhead, identity with which is the ultimate purpose of human existence; this 'Minimum Working Hypothesis' is also the 'Highest Common Factor' of all religions, an idea which Huxley would work out in more detail in his next book.

The Perennial Philosophy (1945)

After the completion of *Time Must Have a Stop*, Huxley began a non-fiction exposition of its underlying philosophy, the *Philosophia Perennis*. This name was of some antiquity (Huxley mistakenly believed it to have been coined by the seventeenth-century philosopher Gottfried Wilhelm Leibniz, although it went even further back, to the sixteenth-century humanist Agostino Steuco), but it had not been employed as uniformly as Huxley believed. As well as the mystics of whom Huxley approved, the term was adopted by adherents of Thomist scholasticism, scholasticism in general, Platonism, positivism, Catholic philosophy and others.[5] As for Huxley, he characterised the perennial philosophy, following Leibniz, as the recognition of a divine reality identical with (some part of) the soul, and the claim that humankind's end and destiny is to apprehend this identity. He claimed, again following Leibniz, that such a view is common to primitive and developed religions in every region of the world. To show this, Huxley's long narrative was illustrated by copious quotations from a range of religious and mystic thinkers gathered with the help of Heard and his colleagues at Trabuco College, and members of the Vedanta Society, which Huxley had recently joined.

The book was divided into twenty-seven chapters, but the main philosophical work was done in the first seven, which between them took up practically half the text. These opening chapters set out Huxley's thinking, little of it original, on (a) the idealistic view that individual selves are identical with the immanent divine essence, (b) the nature of that essence and of the individual personality, and (c) the mode of existence of God in the world and the possibility of apprehending him as truth.

The thrust of the perennial philosophy, that 'the end of human life is contemplation, or the direct and intuitive awareness of God', was totally contrary to most commonly held ideas of the twentieth century, which valorised action, and which assumed that, if contemplation had any purpose at all, it was as a means to purposeful action. Indeed, according to most sophisticated thinkers, the 'minority of contemplatives is perfectly useless and perhaps even harmful to the community which tolerates it'. It is perhaps no accident that the longest chapter outside the first seven concerned our old friends the spiritual exercises as a way of imposing unity and a sense of directed purpose onto humanity.

He marshalled a variety of saints and holy men in quotation and in contemporary report, to represent a diverse selection of creeds, though with a bias towards Hinduism, Mahayana and Zen Buddhism, Taoism and particularly the mystical fringes of Catholicism. Protestantism and Islam were less prominent, the latter represented only by the Sufi sect. Huxley used his immense erudition to good effect, for example effortlessly and apparently casually teasing apart apparently similar statements by Wordsworth and St Bernard to show how the former, as a 'nature-worshipper', is of the world but does not seek to go beyond it, while the latter contemplates nature only as a means to an end – the apprehension of God.

On the other hand, his understanding of the religious traditions about which he was writing was relatively slim.[6] Furthermore, in writing the piece he turned off his brilliant sceptical and critical faculties. None of the sages' comments was scrutinised in any detail to see if it made sense. Huxley's line was that the mystic saint knows intuitively that he is in a holy state. But could a novice correctly judge the saint? Huxley gave no reason to suppose he could.

Science, Liberty and Peace (1946)

Written during the summer of 1945, during which the first atomic bombings took place, *Science, Liberty and Peace* is a short and relevant book. The question is how applied science can be used for the benefit of mankind, rather than its oppression and destruction. The book benefits from a straightforward and unfussy tone and its very few digressions into Californian mysticism; even Huxley's trademark suggestions for conferences and organisations were fewer than usual. The first half of the book consisted of diagnosis, with interesting discussions of Gandhi's *satyagraha* and the perverse effects of the combination of applied science and universal education. The real problem with applied science as it is practised, he argued, is that it tends to result in the monopolisation, and therefore abuse, of power. Although applied science is made for man, not man for applied science, still millions of men are sacrificed because of scientific 'progress'. In a memorable Huxleian image, he wrote that:

> the collective mentality of nations … is that of a delinquent boy of fourteen, at once cunning and childish, malevolent and silly, maniacally egotistical, touchy and acquisitive, and at the same time ludicrously boastful and vain.

In the second half he asked how a scientist should move towards the abolition of war. Of course he or she could refuse to take part in research with a military application (the Buddhists' eightfold path includes 'right livelihood'), or could try to develop political institutions to monitor scientific developments. He discussed the second option in some detail, and hoped it would work, although he was pessimistic that it would be allowed to. Huxley's solution to the dilemma was to consider how scientists could individually reduce the likelihood of war. Characteristically, he imagined an international organisation of scientific workers, and wondered how they would proceed were they tasked with avoiding war. Creating more food was the best bet, foreshadowing the 'green revolution', the dramatic increase in agricultural yields by the combination of the application of science and technology to seed production, improved management techniques and new infrastructure, which markedly reduced food shortages and prices in the 1960s.

He wrote eloquently on energy security and the need to diversify from oil-based products, partly because he deplored the supply monopolies created by over-reliance on naturally occurring minerals, which he felt created too much power.

Political economy has since caught up with Huxley with the concept of the 'resource curse', the idea that possession of natural resources will tend to enrich a ruling minority and impoverish the majority of a nation's people, which has been developed since the 1980s.[7]

Fifty years before such talk became the stuff of liberal opinion, Huxley was advocating solar and wind power, which he thought would promote decentralisation and prevent monopolies growing. In the summer of the atomic bomb, he hoped that atomic power could be a force for good (this being some eight years before Eisenhower's Atoms for Peace speech), although he worried that the need for reliable sources of uranium and other radioactive elements, and large power stations, would each increase the tendency towards monopoly of supply, and therefore tend to work against the decentralisation for which he hoped.

Foreword to 1946 reprint of *Brave New World* (1946)

A reissue of *Brave New World* allowed Huxley to revisit the assumptions of what was already a modern classic after a mere fourteen years, because:

> it seems worth while at least to mention the most serious defect in the story, which is this. The Savage is offered only two alternatives, an insane life in Utopia, or the life of a primitive in an Indian village, a life more human in some respects, but in others hardly less queer and abnormal. At the time the book was written, this idea, that human beings are given free will in order to choose between insanity on the one hand and lunacy on the other, was one that I found amusing and regarded as quite possibly true ... Today I feel no wish to demonstrate that sanity is impossible.

To that end, he wrote a short Foreword to the new edition in 1946, which is usually reprinted in modern editions. He now believed that he had a viable positive philosophy to go with the irony and scepticism of previous years. The 'third alternative', which would probably have wrecked the book as a work of art, appears to the modern eye somewhat less plausible than the Savage's other two, and Huxley still gave little idea of how we might get from here to there, but his long search for a desirable destination was now officially over. The Foreword brought together the disparate ideas developed at length in *Time Must Have a Stop*, *The Perennial Philosophy* and *Science, Liberty and Peace*.

> If I were now to rewrite the book, I would offer the Savage a third alternative. Between the Utopian and the primitive horns of his dilemma would be the possibility of sanity … [in a] community [where] economics would be decentralist and Henry-Georgian, politics Kropotkinesque and co-operative. Science and technology would be used as though, like the Sabbath, they had been made for man, not (as at present and still more so in the Brave New World) as though man were to be adapted and enslaved to them. Religion would be the conscious and intelligent pursuit of man's Final End, the unitive knowledge of the immanent Tao or Logos, the transcendent Godhead or Brahman.

In this passage, Huxley was signalling to a very wide audience (the readership of his most successful work) his dissatisfaction with standard solutions to the problems of the world, not only by espousing the perennial philosophy, but also by citing the minor if not forgotten figures of George and Kropotkin. Henry George (1839–97) was an American economist, author of *Progress and Poverty*, who argued that although everyone should own what he or she creates, the natural world (and most particularly land) should be common property. Peter Kropotkin (1842–1921) was a Russian anarchist and geographer, author of *Mutual Aid*, as well as the article on Anarchism in the *Encyclopaedia Britannica*, Huxley's favourite book.

He remained fascinated with the infrastructure of *Brave New World*, and devoted a few pages to updating his account of propaganda – naturally enough, since wartime communications had reached new levels of effectiveness – musing on the ways in which a revolution in human nature was within reach of politicians and scientists which would allow them to implant the love of servitude in the population, a topic that he would continue to research until his death. The four essential tools for this propagandist revolution, according to Huxley, were methods of suggestion (especially infant conditioning and the use of drugs), a science of human difference (allowing people to be assigned to the job most suited to their capabilities), a drug such as soma to act as a harmless substitute for alcohol or heroin, and a system of eugenics. He now averred that the society which he located six centuries in the future could actually be in place by the end of the twentieth century.

Ape and Essence (1948)

In his next novel, Huxley applied his pre-war pessimism to the post-war era. *Ape and Essence* was his first major post-war work, and rather stuns the reader into submission. Huxley was always prone to bad taste, but *Ape and Essence* provided no elegant contrast, and no relief.

The title was another adaptation of Shakespeare, from *Measure for Measure* where Isabella is trying to persuade Angelo to show mercy to her brother Claudio:

> But man, proud man,
> Dressed in a little brief authority,
> Most ignorant of what he's most assur'd,

(His glassy Essence) like an angry Ape
Plays such fantastic tricks before high heaven,
As makes the Angels weep: who with our spleens,
Would all themselves laugh mortal.

Most ignorant of what he is most assured – the paradox of this line appealed to Huxley. It is also another expression of the wearisome condition: man is an ape even when in authority and at his most civilised. This speech certainly interested him at this period; Sebastian had already quoted it in full in the Epilogue to *Time Must Have a Stop*.

Huxley struggled with the immense pessimism of the story; impossible to render realistically. His solution placed the material at arm's length. The novel begins with a first-person account of movie scriptwriters trying to find a story for a new film; this short preface (thirty-two pages) opens with the news of Gandhi's assassination, connecting the narrative to the problems of the present (dating the action to 31 January 1948, when the news would have hit the newspapers; this was added after Huxley had finished most of the book). There is some light-hearted satire behind the scenes of the movie world (reminiscent of Billy Wilder's *Sunset Boulevard* of 1950), before the narrator and his buddy Bob find a rejected manuscript of a film treatment, *Ape and Essence* by one William Tallis, who lives in Huxleyish seclusion in a desert ranch. Interest piqued, the narrator and Bob drive out to the ranch, only to find Tallis's landlady and her large and picturesque family, who inform them that he had died six weeks ago. The rest of the book consists of Tallis's 'treatment' of *Ape and Essence*.

It is clear from the preface that Tallis is a misanthrope (possibly Huxley mildly spoofing himself), but even so the reader is likely to be surprised at the darkness of the work. The treatment is set in 2108, in a terrible future, some generations after World War III. Dr Alfred Poole, a scientist from New Zealand, whose remoteness saved it from destruction, sets out to explore the nuclear-ravaged world. In California, he is captured by members of a vicious civilisation of survivors. They are deformed mutants, who now have sex only in season; those who preserve their sexual drive all year round are buried alive. Eunuch priests orchestrate the worship of Belial; the Arch-Vicar of Belial, a cross between Dr Obispo and Mustapha Mond, explains the new reality to Poole.

In the Arch-Vicar's view the only explanation for people's destructive actions is diabolic possession, and this applies not only to his own post-apocalyptic society, but also to the pre-apocalypse society in which Huxley and his readers lived. According to the Arch-Vicar's warped theology, Nationalism and Progress (capitalised) were introduced by the Devil for mankind to worship in the nineteenth century, and those early successes led to more and more dangerous wars, until a nuclear holocaust.

Ape and Essence expressed Huxley's philosophy that the 'forces' of history could and should be reduced to the actions of individuals. This view – which in most hands would have produced a positive outcome – led to a strong pessimism in conjunction with Huxley's observation that individuals neglect their duty to resist violence and evil, because the majority of people are slaves to religiosity, whether this is instantiated as nationalism or ideology or scientific progress. At first sight this appears to be something of a mystery, in that human history tells people that their beliefs are not in their own interests. It is obvious from their environment, their culture, their newspapers and their books that the conflicts created by disputes over the rightness or wrongness of quasi-religions can only lead to warfare. Their adherence to ideologies leads directly to slaughter and destruction, yet people persist in their beliefs. How can this be explained except as a case of mass diabolic possession? Poole's escape from the dreadful civilisation of Los Angeles is too equivocal to undermine the Arch-Vicar's impressively cogent analysis; like *Brave New World*, *Ape and Essence* gave no third option of hope.

Themes and Variations (1950)

Themes and Variations is an extremely impressive group of essays written between 1943 and 1950, exploring in the most part the hinterland between art and religion, showing how the best of human achievement sometimes came close to expressing the great truths Huxley had tried to set out in *The Perennial Philosophy*, but more usually fell short. There were eight pieces in total, with the first and the last rather unbalancing the collection.

Of the other six, the greatest is 'Variations on El Greco' (the second major essay he had published on that artist, this one having appeared in *Life* magazine in 1950), in which Huxley explored the quality of El Greco's mystical vision in terms of the forms he used in his art. He located El Greco's style somewhere between Byzantine and Venetian, 'neither flat nor fully three-dimensional'. There was a lack of depth in the spaces in which El Greco crammed human figures below and divine ones above: 'On earth, as in heaven, there is hardly room to swing a cat.' His vision was 'curiously oppressive and disquieting', yet, by virtue of its brilliant coherent unity and harmony, it still suggested implicitly the possibility of union with the Spirit that El Greco had failed to express explicitly.

'Variations on [Piranesi's] *The Prisons*' and 'Variations on Goya' (both of which had been Forewords to other books) discussed the lack of spiritual consolation in those artists' sombre works, while 'Variations on a Baroque Tomb' praised the seventeenth-century mortuary sculptors whose splendidly realised figures of death showed a realism about man's place in the universe, expressing, as Piranesi and Goya did not, *both* the desolation of death *and* the consolation of what will follow.

The opening essay of the collection, 'Variations on a Philosopher', is substantial enough to be a book in itself (twice as long as *Science, Liberty and Peace*), taking up over half of *Themes and Variations*. It initiated the collection's exploration of the relation between mind and body, using the philosopher Maine de Biran in the same way as Huxley had already treated Père Joseph in *Grey Eminence*, that is to say, novelistically and forensically. Having said that, the scene-setting narrative with which the essay began was dispensable and quickly forgotten as Huxley got into the analysis of Biran's journal, the main point of interest. Biran was an acute introspective observer, and Huxley found much insight in his (Biran's) chronicling of the most irrational and ignoble aspects of his experience. In particular, Biran's aches and pains (he was a sickly man) allowed Huxley to emphasise the dependence of the mind upon the body and the situatedness of psychological and rational processes. He argued from this that the exploration of the perennial philosophy demands more than an awareness of our own internal states – the whole point is to unify our experience with that of the Spirit, and the intrusion of our physical states into our mental lives will prevent that happening, however unworldly we imagine ourselves to be. He complained that Biran should have studied mesmerism to get an account of the potential breadth of influence on the mind, although the reader does feel that, as in the essay on El Greco, Huxley was anachronistically imposing his own concerns.

The final essay, 'The Double Crisis', first published in 1948, was the only purely political essay in the collection. Here he argued that the world's crisis existed on two levels, a political and economic one at the higher level, and a demographic and ecological one at the lower. Nationalism and militarism were the real dangers, and there seemed to be no way of implementing the necessary sacrifices to address the more fundamental lower-level crisis. He urged a greater concentration on the degradation of the environment:

> if, presumptuously imagining that we can 'conquer' Nature, we continue to live on our planet like a swarm of destructive parasites – we condemn ourselves and our children to misery

and deepening squalor and the despair that finds expression in the frenzies of collective violence.

The Devils of Loudun (1952)

Collective violence was the subject of Huxley's next work. *Ape and Essence* had introduced the notion of mass diabolic possession to 'explain' humankind's apparent death wish; in *The Devils of Loudun*, Huxley carried out his third foray into fictionalised history to tell 'one of the most fantastically strange stories in all French history'.[8] The story of how a French priest, Urbain Grandier, came to be accused of being the agent of the demoniac possession of a small convent of Ursuline nuns in the town of Loudun in 1632–4, of how political and personal enmity led to Grandier's condemnation and torture, and of the mental degradation of a saintly and scholarly Jesuit who took part in the exorcism, is told with verve, interspersed with speculations and reflections that brought the history up to date.

Huxley was at pains to emphasise both the thinness of our veneer of modernity, and the vast psychological distance between mid-twentieth-century man, secular, positivist and technological, and the superstitious, religious dogmatics of three hundred years earlier. Yes, it is hard to imagine a community lapsing into such a madness today – but Huxley drew the parallels between the events of 1634 and the Stalinist show trials and even the concentration camps, each fresh in the contemporary reader's memory.

Interestingly, although hysteria about devils and demons appears to be a perfect metaphor for the McCarthyist hunts for communist traitors in the US, which at the time of writing were in full swing (and whose effects were certainly felt in Hollywood at the time he was writing *The Devils*, for example by his black-listed friend Burgess Meredith), Huxley does not seem to have meant the work in this way. Joseph McCarthy, the sort of narrow-minded populist that Huxley despised, is absent from his essays and published letters. In contrast, Arthur Miller's *The Crucible* of 1953 famously used the similar story of the witch-hunts in Salem, Massachusetts to criticise McCarthy obliquely.

As with the earlier works, Huxley used his novelist's talents to bring the period and characters alive for the reader, no doubt at the cost of historical veracity. For example, here he is sketching a character upon his first appearance, cutting through the historical detail to create a memorable caricature:

> For a man of only forty-one, M. de Laubardemont had gone far. His career was a demonstration of the fact that, in certain circumstances, crawling is a more effective means of locomotion than walking upright, and that the best crawlers are also the deadliest biters. All his life Laubardemont had systematically crawled before the powerful and bitten the defenceless.

He wrote with a brilliant irony, and amid the torture, hysteria and malevolence there is some pure laugh-out-loud comedy in Grandier's easy conquests, the rivalries in the town, the credulity of the exorcists and the antics of the nuns. They performed great physical feats, passing their legs over their shoulders and round their heads, and doing the splits. 'Reading ... accounts of the nuns' performances,' Huxley comments drily, 'one is forced to the conclusion that, as well as *naturaliter Christiana*, the feminine soul is *naturaliter Drum-Majoretta*.'

Grandier himself, as Huxley portrays him, is a pugnacious sensualist whose womanising and arrogance eventually alienate an important faction in Loudun leading to his fall, condemnation and horrific torture (Huxley spares no details). The head of the nuns, Sœur Jeanne, is a lying, hypocritical attention-seeker. They are each fine creations, appalling yet recognisably human at the same time. Jeanne's credulity, self-delusion and willingness to go along with the anti-Grandier faction allow the plot to grow from small beginnings, eventually involving the king and a daily audience of tourists keen to watch hysterical nuns spouting obscenities. It is certainly an extraordinary story, and Huxley evokes the rough-and-tumble world of seventeenth-century religious rivalry and small-town politics, in which no holds were barred and no persons respected.

His chief interest, however, is the Jesuit Father Jean-Joseph Surin, who only appears in Loudun four months after Grandier's execution in order to exorcise Sœur Jeanne, and who is barely relevant to the main action of the possessions and the judicial murder of Grandier (Surin is absent from most other dramatic versions of the possessions). The saintly Surin, whose 'faith was gluttonous and indiscriminate', breaks under the strain, and for two decades becomes insane and paralysed in body, unable even to change his clothes without enormous pain. The interaction of mind and body and the immanent soul are Huxley's interest here, and he traces the evolution of Surin's thought (he was the author of a number of works of theology and poetry) as he gradually comes to terms with his own personal psychological 'devils' – he had misguidedly translated his desire to be one with God to a fanatical self-loathing.

As an interesting postscript, Huxley wrote a small appendix for *The Devils of Loudun* discussing methods of self-transcendence, including immersion in a crowd, sexual debauchery and – most interestingly, given his later thought – intake of alcohol or drugs. He concluded that self-transcendence could lead one to an understanding of immanent Being, but was more likely simply to alienate one from the given world. His next book, *The Doors of Perception* (a phrase that he had already used towards the end of *The Devils of Loudun*), would modify this thesis along more optimistic lines.

Thought

Huxley's conversion to a more religious point of view had been driven by a long-standing urge to create a positive philosophy, and by his engagement with the disarmament movement. His journey to America had a number of important effects. Most notably, it removed him from a theatre of war. That not only reduced the privations upon him, but also made the political pressures less immediate, allowing a more considered approach (though the flip side was that it distanced him from the practical detail of implementing pacifism in the 1930s and 1940s). It changed his intellectual circle. Whereas in Europe he was intimate with a fractious group of poets, writers and artists either of independent means or living by their art, in the US he was more interested in learning from salaried academics on university campuses. It also separated his social circle from his intellectual circle, as now he socialised in Hollywood with a few towering thinkers and artists (such as Stravinsky), and many more brilliant but not necessarily political communicators (such as Chaplin or Harpo Marx). It increased the influence of Gerald Heard, whose contacts additionally led to close friendships with Christopher Isherwood and Krishnamurti. Most important of all, it increased Huxley's confidence to find himself lauded as a genius.

This confluence of forces allowed him to follow through the philosophy of *Eyeless in Gaza* and *Ends and Means* without hindrance. The scepticism, doubt and nuance which were tools of the trade for the public intellectual in Europe were less and less use to Huxley as he tried to make the case for peace as robustly as he could. Furthermore, the ideological tramlines of left and right which set the tone of European thought were taken far less seriously in the US, where neither out-of-the-box nor off-the-wall thinking were disqualifications for being taken seriously.

What strikes the reader of the late Huxley works is the complete suppression of his early scepticism. He retained a powerful respect for science throughout his career, but never espoused the positivistic dogma that science is the only source of knowledge or value, and certainly never believed that science was a tool that could only be used for good. He also took his scientific attitude to imply an open mind, but in later life this gradually warped into a decided lack of discrimination and an unwillingness (perhaps an inability) to be critical about anything but hard science, with the result that he took seriously all sorts of studies and therapies, from dianetics to parapsychology, from the Bates Method to the Alexander Technique, and consorted with serious scientists, pseudo-scientists and mediums on equal terms. A characteristic letter of 1954, to his old friend Dr J.B. Rhine who ran a parapsychology laboratory at Duke University in Durham, North Carolina, shows the two sides of Huxley's character in two maddeningly inconsistent paragraphs, credulous in the first, scathing of uncritical belief in the second:

> California, as you know, is full of oddities. I saw one of them, the other day, in the shape of two aircraft engineers who have been experimenting with deep hypnosis and have come up, in one case, with a gift of tongues. I listened to the tape recording and the foreign language certainly doesn't sound like the gibberish of ordinary glossolalia. Indian students at the university say they recognize it as the dialect of Orissa. The engineers are now engaged in trying to find a scholar who is thoroughly familiar with this brand of Bengali, and who will tell them if this is really an utterance in a language with which the speaker, in his normal state, has had no acquaintance or contact. It probably isn't anything. But if it were, how exceedingly odd it would be.

> Meanwhile I am appalled by the superstitious passion for marvels displayed even by intelligent and well-educated men. I am thinking of a doctor friend of ours who, through a medium, consults his defunct professors and obtains from them, naturally enough, a complete confirmation of his own views about medicine and treatment! And I know of others who have just gone off, on a tip given by the spirits, to look for buried treasure in Arizona – in the teeth of the statement, in every serious history

of the Southwest, that the aborigines did no mining and the early Jesuits and Franciscans either none or very little. Needless to say no appeal to facts or reason is of any avail. What may be called the Baconian-pyramidological-cryptographic-spiritualist-theosophical syndrome afflicts a large percentage of the human race, who get so much fun out of their mental derangement that they don't want, at any cost, to be cured.[9]

The reader of Huxley's American works must be prepared for such inconsistency.

Thou Art That

The need to resolve the questions of peace had led to pacifism, and the need for a metaphysical foundation for pacifism had led to mysticism. Now Huxley followed the practical imperative to flesh out his philosophy – billed not as *his* philosophy, but as the highest common factor in all the world's religions, first sketched in *Grey Eminence* and set out in detail in *The Perennial Philosophy*.

What was this magic factor which would solve the world's problems? Mysticism, for Huxley, was an intuition of *unity*. One felt oneself *at one* with a more comprehensive reality – Huxley used many names for this, including Mind at Large, and the Brahman (a Hindu term for the origin or Divine Ground of the phenomenal universe, also referred to as the Godhead). In order for there to be goodness in the world, and in order for it to thrive, it should be the destiny and final end for man to immerse himself in this unity, which seemed to Huxley to entail the rejection of sources of plural experience. The wearisome condition was an illusion, or using a term common to many Indian philosophies, *maya*. This then meant, quite simply, that one should work to immerse and ultimately lose one's self in the unitive medium, which he equated with God.

Already in the 1920s (*Those Barren Leaves*) Huxley had toyed with the potential for mysticism to unify man's multiplicity, and in *The Perennial Philosophy* he explored that thought in detail. We can promiscuously identify ourselves with a tremendous variety of experiences, and as a result have complex and indeed contradictory personalities, but Huxley argued that the experiences of the mystical saints he had studied showed that people could 'become better and quite other than their own selves'. Acceptance of the wearisome condition was a prerequisite for enlightenment; one needed to be conscious of oneself in time and the world in order to advance into eternity. If one failed to achieve that consciousness, one would remain mired in time, and be stuck in a life of desire, craving, sorrow and pain. Hence Eustace Barnack in *Time Must Have a Stop* could not bring himself to leave behind the glories of art and architecture, of romantic love and sensual pleasure to accept enlightenment.

Huxley was particularly taken with the idealism that made its appearance in India with the Upanishads, philosophical texts of great antiquity. This was expressed in a series of 'great sayings', from which Huxley was prone to quote '*tat tvam asi*', usually translated as 'Thou Art That'. This expressed the truth that, in Upanishadic terms, the Atman is the Brahman, the Atman being the self or ego. To say that the Atman is the Brahman is therefore to say the self is the ultimate ground of reality, or that reality is basically pure consciousness.

In European idealism – as for instance in Plato or Kant – this idea is usually taken to mean that ultimate reality is unknowable, and that the material world as apprehended by the self is not intrinsically real. When it is combined with the Buddhist idea that the end of existence is to annihilate the self, then it is better expressed as saying that the self should be swallowed by the ultimate reality of which it is an aspect. The drop should become part of the ocean.

No particular mode of understanding – science, common sense, religion, art, literature – can encompass everything.

They can at best give a partial, warped and probably misleading view of reality. The philosopher must try to understand reality from as many points of view as possible, and still be aware that they will remain jointly inadequate until the Atman is dissolved into the Brahman.

To achieve true knowledge, therefore, the individual must perceive that the self and the world are identical. The Brahman, being oneness, cannot be apprehended by the senses. Knowledge that purports to be about the material world understood separately from the self or the Godhead (knowledge which we usually refer to as science) is fundamentally incomplete. Huxley argued this on philosophical grounds, and also on the basis of phenomenological analyses of experience in pieces such as *The Art of Seeing* and 'Variations on a Philosopher'.

Upanishadic idealism had an immediate effect on Huxley's own philosophy of multiple realities which had been the cornerstone of so much of his work, especially in the 1920s. Now he understood reality to be *transcendent* in important ways, although consistent with the fragmented *experience* of the wearisome condition, because it was *immanent* in all experience.

The environment

The immanence of the Godhead entailed the need for respect for all things. Huxley gestured towards the environmentalism of the perennial philosophy explicitly in *The Devils of Loudun*, when he drew a parallel between East and West in the 'almost Taoist spirit' in which Christ talked about the lilies of the field. The environment, in its broadest sense, has meaning and value of its own, derived from the Godhead, over and above that which humans derive from it. We must reach out to God through His creation, 'blessedly other'; in contrast, he deplored the view, stemming from mainstream Catholicism as well as Cartesian mechanistic philosophy, that the value of creation, or the environment, or other creatures and objects, depends entirely on the value imputed to them. The lilies of the field toil not, neither do they spin, but that does not make them valueless. Father Surin rejected the world and his own body, and only late in life repented of his mistake. It is only 'through the *datum* of nature that we can hope to receive the *donum* of Grace' ('*datum*' = the given, '*donum*' = gift).

The world is given, and, as the Zen masters advised, we should not try to hunt or create the truth, but cease to cherish our own opinions. The world is as it is, and to be understood and explored as such; it is not meant to conform to our preconceived notions or intellectually reached ideals (in *The Perennial Philosophy* Huxley quoted a parable from Chuang Tzu, the Taoist sceptic of the fourth century BC, in which two rulers try to refashion Chaos in their own image, only to destroy it). He argued that man should not be nature's master but her 'intelligently docile collaborator'. God is in the world, and it is essential that we should neither reject the world, nor try to conquer it. Science and technology should be tools for understanding our environment, not for dominating it.

World, body and self: the Sheldonian theory

We are present in nature, and are embodied in it; this was a vital fact that Huxley felt had been overlooked in both religion and secular philosophy, which concentrated on the mind rather than the body. Huxley had been impressed with the psychologist Ernst Kretschmer who classified body types and mental types, and who had flirted with the eugenic policies of the Nazis. But eventually Huxley found himself convinced by the work of W.H. Sheldon. He had come across Sheldon's theory of correlations between body types and mental types in the 1930s, but on reading *The Varieties of Human Physique* some time in 1942 or 1943, he began to recommend it as a profound contribution to psychology. Sheldon's theory was empirically based, but even so the correlations seem empty and unmotivated. It rarely features in modern academic psychology, and it seems to have no explanatory function. Nevertheless, Huxley went overboard on it, and it featured prominently in many of his works from the mid-1940s onward.

The Sheldonian scheme can be summarised in tabular form; the descriptions are taken from *The Perennial Philosophy*:

Physical type	Notes	Correlated mental type	Notes
Endomorph	Predominantly soft and rounded and may easily become grossly fat. Has a huge gut. In a real sense, his body is built around the digestive tract.	Viscerotonic	Love of food and of eating in common. Love of comfort and luxury. Love of ceremoniousness. Indiscriminate amiability. Love of people as such. Fear of solitude, craving for affection.
Mesomorph	Hard, big-boned and strong-muscled.	Somatotonic	Love of muscular activity, aggressiveness and lust for power. Indifference to pain. Callousness. Love of combat and competition.

Physical type	Notes	Correlated mental type	Notes
Ectomorph	Slender, with small bones and stringy, weak, unemphatic muscles. Over-sensitive, with a relatively unprotected nervous system.	Cerebrotonic	Over-alert, over-sensitive introvert. Little desire to dominate. Passion for privacy. Nervous, shy, tensely inhibited, unpredictably moody. Extremely, almost insanely sexual, but hardly ever tempted to drink.

In *Time Must Have a Stop*, the three Barnacks are modelled directly on Sheldon's scheme – Sebastian is a cerebrotonic, his father John is somatotonic and his Uncle Eustace viscerotonic. Neither Sheldon nor Huxley were saying that the world divides neatly into these types, so everyone is either Mr Pickwick or John Wayne or Charles Hawtrey (or female equivalent); rather, everyone partakes to some degree in these types, and on occasion one finds people who fit one of them almost exactly. This doesn't make the theory any more sensible, except by transforming it from something that is palpably false into an empty truism. Nevertheless, Huxley announced to a probably somewhat bemused E.S.P. Haynes that this was 'the first serious advance in the science of man since the days of Aristotle'.[10]

In *The Perennial Philosophy*, Huxley used the Sheldonian scheme to create an ethnography of theology in which somatotonics were the cause of social upheaval, while cerebrotonics were naturally inclined to contemplation and approved of monotheism. But cerebrotonics could go too far, believing (like Calvin) so strongly in their own intellectual constructions that they lost their grip of reality. The power-loving somatotonic and the gluttonous viscerotonic, living more deeply in the world, are more likely to be idolatrous, seeing God everywhere in the world but failing to apprehend his immanent nature.

Although it is well-nigh impossible to see what chapter VIII of *The Perennial Philosophy*, where this ethnography is sketched, contributed to his argument as a whole, it is one of many examples of Huxley's thinking about the relation between God and the world leading to exploration of the relations between mind and body (as he pointed out, Catholic and Mahayana Buddhist doctrine alike insist that, in order to move towards enlightenment, embodiment is essential).

He thought it would be miraculous if there were no correlation between the physical and the mental. Eustace Barnack's epicurean weariness is caused by the gradual failure of his obese body. The nuns and hysterics of *The Devils of Loudun* mortify their bodies and see demons. *The Art of Seeing* demands the simultaneous treatment of the mental faculty of perception, the organs of sight and the body as a whole. The philosophical limitations of Maine de Biran were directly related to his poor health; how could he become a contemplative if his body was constantly intruding into his thought via pain? The pioneering anti-individualist philosophers of the American and British tradition, such as Willard Quine, Ludwig Wittgenstein and Gilbert Ryle, focused on social norms and the public fixing of meaning and reference, but Huxley was one of the few English-language philosophers who tried to explain the centrality of embodiment (embodiment was generally taken more seriously in Continental philosophy, as in the work of Merleau-Ponty and Heidegger, but Huxley was more comfortably in the Anglo-Saxon analytic tradition).

Apprehension of the Godhead and the morally good individual

Huxley's thought now had two aspects. The proper end of existence was to apprehend the Godhead, but he also wanted a spiritually educated people to perform morally good actions in the world. In *The Perennial Philosophy* and elsewhere, he wrestled with the problem, raised in his PPU pamphlets in the 1930s, of trying to coordinate action and make individual acts of goodness effective. He raised the idea of charity as disinterested, humble, selfless acts of love, and claimed such acts had a legitimacy all their own precisely because charity could not compel itself. Love is always voluntary, a 'thing of perfect freedom' (quoting the German Anabaptist Hans Denck), and so contrasts with the organised and exploitative lovelessness of global finance, mass production and mass distribution that he had satirised in *Brave New World*.

Yet Huxley's individualism meant that he could not blame institutions and impersonal social forces for the problems of the world. No one is coerced into submitting these structures at the point of a gun. One cannot absolve oneself by blaming the institution. There is no excuse not to do good even if all the social and institutional incentives pointed the other way.

As Propter says in *After Many a Summer*, at least some of the causes of disasters and hatreds:

> are generally under the control of the people who suffer the disasters or are the object of the hatred. In some measure they are directly or indirectly responsible. Directly, by the commission of stupid or malicious acts. Indirectly, by the omission to be as intelligent and compassionate as they might be.

Anthony Beavis had argued in *Eyeless in Gaza* that 'Nations won't change their national policies unless and until people change their private policies. All governments, even Hitler's, even Stalin's, even Mussolini's, are representative.'

It is of course hard to anticipate the undesirable consequences of our actions, and one can never know exactly what will follow from our decisions, but this is no get-out – there are some rough guides:

> though it is impossible to foresee the remoter consequences of any given course of action, it is by no means impossible to foresee, in the light of past historical experience, the sorts of consequences that are likely, in a general way, to follow certain sorts of acts.
>
> (*Grey Eminence*)

What troubled Huxley was unthinking behaviour, that so few people questioned deeply enough their contribution to the violence in and between societies. Identification with interests wider than one's own, even with something as trivial as a hobby or as precious as love (in *The Devils of Loudun* he called such identification 'horizontal self-transcendence'), was the root of all social benefits (science, philosophy, art) and curses (war, intolerance, persecution). In *Time Must Have a Stop* he wrote that the very people who held society together made up the forces that pushed everyone apart, because of their unthinking support for inconsistent and sometimes vicious ideas: 'Susan and Kenneth and Aunt Alice and all their kind ... were the pillars [of society], but they were also the dynamite; simultaneously the beams and the dryrot.'

But how to steer Susan and Kenneth and Aunt Alice in the right direction? *The Perennial Philosophy*, where it entered into controversy at all, took sides with Mahayana and Zen masters against their Hinayana Buddhist brethren.[11] The purely contemplative

Hinayana were taken to task again and again for failing to realise that God is in the world, and that the aim of contemplation should be to discover, and blend with, the nexus of divine and profane. In surrendering selfhood, we should aim at unity with God as he is in the world; Atman is Brahman. Yet the politically interested reader might wonder how the perennial philosopher could do good in the world. Even the worldlier Mahayanas sounded like withdrawn ascetics on Huxley's account. Where were the Bodhisattvas of the Mahayana tradition, the compassionate saints who laboured in this world for the enlightenment of all beings?

Practically, his mystical philosophy could only propose merging the self with the immanent Godhead. The world looks like a dung-heap 'seen through the dung-coloured spectacles of self-interest', but our perception can be cleansed by becoming more innocent, disinterested and childlike. 'As long as I am this or that, or have this or that, I am not all things and I have not all things' (a quotation from Meister Eckhart, 1260–1327, a German Christian Neoplatonist). The heavenly virtues of humility, patience and charity can be promoted via reason or will, but this is not sufficient; these virtues need to be absorbed into one's self.

He was not generally optimistic that many people would seek such unity. In *Grey Eminence* he linked it with the possibility of what he called 'goodness politics', 'the art of organizing on a large scale without sacrificing the ethical values which emerge only among individuals and small groups'. He did not believe that goodness politics could happen without 'individual training in theocentric theory and contemplative practice' so that the majority of individuals could 'transform their personalities by the only method known to be effective'.

If the optimistic scenario was religiously inspired, so was the pessimism that enveloped Huxley at mid-century, expressed using the religious imagery of demoniac possession. For Huxley, possession was not literal, yet was none the less real. Indeed, he saw it as a primarily secular phenomenon (naturally it would take on a supernatural *appearance* in a society as rigidly religious as seventeenth-century France). Possession is self-made; people welcome 'devils' into themselves. In Loudun, Sœur Jeanne and the Ursuline nuns responded to the exorcists' suggestions; in modern times, people are more likely to be possessed by the evil and wrongdoing of a hated class, nationality or race. It is right and natural for nationalities or ideologies to try to wipe their rivals violently from the map, an effect detectable at all levels of society. The little man just as much as the powerful can satiate his lust for power via support for an imperialistic state.

Evaluating Huxley's mystical thought: saints and sceptics

How defensible is Huxley's later philosophy? It is worth pointing out that, although he often argued that mysticism was a logical conclusion of metaphysical thinking ('the only proved method of transforming personality'), his inquiries became increasingly dogmatic. The foundations of the perennial philosophy had not been laid. He had established to his own satisfaction that mysticism was the only potential solution for the ills of the day, but had followed a train of thought based on his own doubtful assumptions.

His first assumption was that fighting Hitler's Nazis would solve nothing, as bad means could not serve good ends. Second, he assumed that the creation of wealth using technology would simply give nations greater power. Third, if those nations were not made up primarily of morally good people, this power would inevitably be used for aggressive purposes. Fourth, the likely product of modern warfare would be apocalypse and, if not the end of civilisation, at least its abeyance. Fifth, mysticism and spiritual exercises were the only practicable and effective methods of making people morally good. It followed from all that that widespread acceptance of the perennial philosophy was necessary if the world was to be saved for human civilisation. So indeed it did, but his crucial assumptions, each highly controversial to say the least, were asserted almost without defence.

Furthermore, he had not shown that it was feasible for everyone to become morally good. In particular, he had not shown that the perennial philosophy was *true*, either as a description of the relation between mind and reality, or as a method of self-improvement. Even if mysticism is the only possible hope for the world, it does not follow that the world has hope. Huxley was going further than the error of deriving 'ought' from 'is', which David Hume identified in *A Treatise on Human Nature*. Huxley was deriving 'is' from 'ought' – people *ought* to stop war and embrace pacifism, and therefore a mystical reality (the perennial philosophy, the Highest Common Factor) has to be *true*.

Could the mystic experiences and intuitions of the sources of *The Perennial Philosophy* stand up to the rigours of a properly scientific scepticism? Just because one receives an intuition accompanied by a strong sense of its truth, that does not *make* it true. Even if a genuine mystical experience is necessarily accompanied by testament of its own genuineness, a deluded person might mistake some aspect of a hallucination as a certificate of its veracity too.

Huxley could recognise the problem. In *The Devils of Loudun*, he recalled the pious Anabaptist who was inspired by the story of Abraham and Isaac to cut off his brother's head:

> Such teleological suspensions of morality, as Kierkegaard elegantly calls them, are all very well in the Book of Genesis, but not in real life. In real life we have to guard against the gruesome pranks of the maniac within.

Nevertheless, he did not draw what seems to be the obvious conclusion that mystical experiences are indistinguishable from hallucinations. One cannot solipsistically determine the nature of one's own religious or mystical experiences except at the risk of being seriously misled by oneself, or by unfortunate bodily influences upon the mind.

In *The Perennial Philosophy* Huxley pointed out that the traditions of the church and the obedience due to its officers could help prevent the inner maniac going berserk; in this way, institutional religion and intuitive religion counterbalance each other. He also discussed the Quaker practice of consulting with 'weighty Friends' whose experience can help a person decide on the veracity of his or her intuitions. So whatever religious experience one has, one needs to socialise it to make sense of it. But Huxley persisted in believing that solipsistic meditation and contemplation were panaceas for political ills.

Evaluating Huxley's mystical thought: peace and religion

Part of the problem was that Huxley continued to insist, as he had since the 1930s, that only majorities, and overwhelming ones at that, could effect change. He found that the reign of violence would never end until 'this Perennial Philosophy is recognized as the highest factor common to all the world religions'. He criticised the ignorance of theologians, philosophers and scholars about non-Western religions, and demanded that they work to make the commonalities across religions evident.

Yet Huxley's argument still seems the wrong way around. Citing St Paul, he claimed that the tranquillity of contemplation of God, 'the peace that passeth all understanding', can only be found by attempting to create the types of peace that everyone understands – between nations (because warfare eclipses religion), between individuals, and within individuals (because private fears, loves or ambitions, though petty, are still fatal to the contemplative frame of mind). Yet counter-intuitively, on Huxley's account violence appears to be evil not because it causes harm to others, but because it disturbs the potential for order:

> Thou art That; and though That is immortal and impassible, the killing and torturing of individual 'thous' is a matter of cosmic significance, inasmuch as it interferes with the normal and natural relationship between individual souls and the divine eternal Ground of all being. Every violence is, over and above everything else, a sacrilegious rebellion against the divine order.

Did Huxley really want to say that violence and evil are only *contingently* wrong, because they disturb the divine order? Are they not *conceptually* wrong? If they are only contingently wrong, might a Eustace Barnack not reply that there was nothing so special about the divine order that makes it worth sacrificing art and good living for? And if the result was a little violence here and there, then that too might be a sacrifice worth making.

In contrast, Huxley's assessment of orthodox religion was based on its contributions to peace and understanding on the one hand and war and persecution on the other, rather than on examination of doctrine. For example, in *The Devils of Loudun*, he suggested a functional account of institutionalised religion: 'Thou Art That', a fact of consciousness, is communicated by religions by metaphorically embodying the eternal essence of mind as an infinite deity. The religion is therefore an institutional framework which can push the devotee towards an appreciation of the truths of the perennial philosophy, and this is the value of all the different dogmas, symbols, rites and myths that it contains. Religion, like science, was a tool which could be used for human good, or misused.

Therefore we should not be surprised that religion has bad effects as well as good. When it helps the individual forget his own ego and naive view of the universe, then it can help him on the road to enlightenment. On the other hand, it can and often does provoke dangerous and damaging passions, such as fear, righteous indignation, zeal and hatred of the other. Dogmatically pursued, it can sanctify and legitimise vicious behaviour in its name. Verbal statements of theology can be a cause of violence; the vague form of the theological expression is treated with the reverence that should be reserved for the fact it imperfectly expresses.

Words have positive and negative uses. At best, they can frame working hypotheses to help us explore and try to understand the phenomena we encounter. At worst, they crystallise into dogmas, whether religious, political or scientific – at which point they become dangerous. Men group together to defend them. Furthermore, words are necessarily imprecise. *The Perennial Philosophy* pointed out that a phrase like 'God is Love' is devalued when the term 'Love' is used to cover not just deep theological apprehension, but also the romances on a cinema screen and support for a football team. 'Ambiguity of vocabulary leads to confusion of thought' allowing people to say and even believe that they are serving God while really 'serving Mammon, Mars or Priapus'. And conversely, confusion about metaphysics leads to confusion about words. 'An overvaluation of happenings in time and an undervaluation of the everlasting, timeless fact of eternity' leads to 'bloody disputes over the interpretation of the not very adequate and often conflicting records'.

Huxley's views of the tyranny of words partly explains the appeal of the politics and history of the seventeenth century, the cusp between the Renaissance and the Enlightenment. Science was not yet understood as a practice or discipline. Even the brilliant physicist and mathematician Sir Isaac Newton wrote copiously on alchemy, and developed his mechanical system to express the order that he believed God had imposed upon the world. The vital issues of the nature of the truths of science became at that time a serious spiritual problem. In the 1946 Foreword to *Brave New World*, he argued that:

> the unimaginable horrors of the Thirty Years War actually taught men a lesson, and for more than a hundred years the politicians and generals of Europe consciously resisted the temptation to use their military resources to the limits of destructiveness or (in the majority of conflicts) to go on fighting until the enemy was totally annihilated.

In the context of the 1940s, with the shadow of nuclear weaponry over the world, this was a poignant reflection.

Theological warfare of the type endemic in the seventeenth century was down to intolerance of alternative expression, whether religious or scientific; in fact, peace follows tolerance, which follows from a proper irreverence towards words. In the twentieth century, Huxley argued, debate over political ideology had followed a similar course to seventeenth-century debate, but without the restraints of humanism, honour or tradition which were in place during the time of Père Joseph.

Huxley's assertion that all religions and pseudo-religions should be discarded in favour of the perennial philosophy, otherwise 'no amount of political planning, no economic blue-prints however ingeniously drawn, can prevent the recrudescence of war and revolution', was unfortunate for two reasons. First, it seems extremely unlikely that this is true, and Huxley provided no argument for it. Furthermore, if one rejected all religions for the reasons Huxley gave, why not go on to reject religion *tout court*? Indeed, if the perennial philosophy was the only factor common to all religions, and all religions were unsatisfactory and dangerous, one might quite reasonably conclude that the perennial philosophy was unsatisfactory and dangerous too. The perennial philosophy might be the cankerous core that creates all the problems.

Second, Huxley's universalism put him in contradiction with himself. 'Theological imperialism is a menace to permanent world peace', he said – yet in the very next sentence added that 'the reign of violence will never come to an end until … most human beings accept the same, true philosophy of life'. If the latter assertion was not theological imperialism, it came jolly close, and, as Huxley himself had eloquently argued many times, religious demonisation and ideological negativity open up a space for evil acts in the cause of a supposed good. This was Huxley's diagnosis of the political misery of the mid-twentieth century, and yet here he was, the great opponent of holy or political war, using the same dangerous rhetorical devices.

All in all, the new philosophy was motivated by hope rather than reason, was not particularly consistent and was undermined by Huxley's pessimism. If there was little hope of people apprehending the identity of the Atman and the Brahman, what was the use of Huxley's writings, or of anyone reading them? Despite the extensive research that went into *The Perennial Philosophy*, a further ingredient was required before Huxley's late philosophy achieved maturity.

7

Techno-utopian, 1953–63

Life

The Doors of Perception, which describes Huxley's first experiment with the psychedelic drug mescalin (usually known as mescaline, illegal in the US since 1970), is probably the most read of his non-fiction works. For Huxley himself, this research linked a number of strands of his thought: the socially beneficial use of science, the effects of states of a person's body on their psychology, and the facilitation of mystical experience and contemplative understanding across the population. Simply, Huxley hypothesised that psychedelic drugs, if harmless and non-addictive, could engineer the widespread experience of immanent oneness with the Divine Ground of Being which would enable progressive politics to emerge.

New attitudes towards drugs which developed in the 1960s sent this very well-meant work into a completely different direction. Huxley, whose liking for popular music was not far off nil, would probably have been horrified by the posthumous lionising he received in the counterculture, although equally he would have found much of which to approve in the hippies' peace agenda. Fundamentally he saw his work as a serious investigation into mystical understanding, not 'turn on, tune in, drop out' self-indulgence and hedonism. Only rarely did he allow himself to joke about the topic, as when he mused on the possibility that good sense might break out if his acquaintance Timothy Leary (later a hippie icon) could smuggle some LSD into a summit between Kennedy and Khrushchev.

In 1953, Huxley read an article about psychological medicine by Humphry Osmond, an Englishman practising in Canada, and promptly invited him to California. When Osmond attended a meeting of the American Psychiatric Association in Los Angeles, he took him up on the invitation, bringing mescalin with him. On 4 May, Huxley took the drug under Osmond's supervision. Although he did not achieve the De Quinceyish visions for which he was hoping (he was to the end of his life disappointed at his inability to visualise with either mescalin or later with LSD), he did find himself experiencing naked existence, 'manifested Suchness' – what Eckhart called *Istigkeit*, or Is-ness. He wrote *The Doors* quickly, and it sold well. A further experiment took place in early 1955, this time with Heard and others in tow, leading to a follow-up piece, *Heaven and Hell*.

In November 1953, the Huxleys, following in their son's footsteps, applied for American citizenship. The FBI already had a file on Huxley, who had spoken at a number of communist-funded peace conferences (Huxley had no time for communism, but in the paranoid McCarthyite years, even a tenuous association was bad enough), but what did for his application was his answering 'no' to the question of whether he would be prepared to bear arms in the US Army. If he had been prepared to cite religious reasons, even that would not have been an obstacle. But he refused to hide behind faith – his reasons were absolutely rational. There would have been serious trouble had the application been refused (he might ultimately have been deported), but the judge instead kindly adjourned the proceedings. They were never renewed, and so technically held in abeyance for the rest of their lives.

April 1954 found the Huxleys once more visiting Europe. Maria had had little remission from her cancer, and was not in the best state to travel across the US, from New York to France, then Egypt, Lebanon, Israel, Cyprus, Greece and Italy. By the time they arrived in Rome, she was tired and thin; she had a series of psychotherapy sessions with an Italian acquaintance of theirs whom they had met in California, Laura Archera. Back in France Aldous managed to work on a new novel, but Maria was by now so ill that immediate return to America was advised. Extraordinarily, while they were awaiting passage on a ship, Aldous hopped over the English Channel for a short stay with his brother Julian; it seems that he was either unaware of the extent of Maria's illness, or unable to face it.[1] Eventually they sailed in August.

The next few months were spent working. Maria's health continued to decline, but although she confided in friends (and even her cook), she insisted that Aldous was told very little. A letter to Matthew from Aldous dated 5 December 1954, for example, mentioned that Maria was having X-rays, but most of the letter contained advice gleaned from Osmond about how to make sure small children, 'unequipped, psychologically, to deal with large numbers of people', enjoy Christmas parties. Another to friends on 10 January 1955 discussed Maria's treatment, which 'achieved the desired results'. He also described her recurrent and painful lumbago, but 'in spite of everything we are happy'. On the 22nd, Maria had come home from hospital fitted with a brace; 'some liver trouble was found; but the doctor seems to think that much of this will clear up spontaneously as the result of helping the back'. A letter to Matthew on the 30th, however, described a relapse, a further stay in hospital, anti-infection drugs, nightly fevers and another course of painful X-rays.

The letters over the next week all mentioned Maria's deterioration, but not to the exclusion of other family news, details of the progress of Aldous's work (especially the completion of the novel, entitled *The Genius and the Goddess*, for serialisation in *Harper's Magazine*), and excited discussions of scientific developments with Osmond. His letter to old friend Peggy Kiskadden on 5 February talked of Maria's worsening condition, but on that day he was told that she had no more than a few days to live. He immediately wrote to Maria's sister Jeanne that 'if we are to believe the doctors, there is no hope. She will be coming back to the house the day after tomorrow as she will be happier at home.'[2]

Maria did indeed return home on Monday 7 February,[3] and Laura Archera visited that afternoon to try to avert her nausea with hypnosis. Aldous tried hypnotherapy which seems to have been successful in preventing vomiting and allowing her to take food. She was able to recognise Matthew, who flew in from New York on Tuesday, but barely able to communicate with her sister Suzanne when she arrived on Wednesday. Aldous stayed with Maria for long hours, trying to contact the deeper levels of her mind, encouraging her long love of the desert and light, trying to conjure her 'abiding sense of divine immanence'. Maria's aged mother arrived later in the week, finding Maria calm.

Maria finally succumbed in the early hours of Saturday 12 February, at the age of fifty-six, in the presence of Aldous, Matthew and Peggy Kiskadden. Aldous spoke to her for the final three hours, holding her with his left hand on her head and his right hand on her solar plexus 'creat[ing] a kind of vital circuit', describing the beauty of the mystical reality he and she had been exploring, and repeating mantras and wisdom from the *Tibetan Book of the Dead*. 'Peace now. Peace, love, joy *now*. Being *now*.' And, at the end, 'Let go, let go. Forget the body, leave it lying here; it is of no importance now. Go forward into the light.' At six o'clock, her pulse ceased. She was buried two days later, in the presence of her family, Gerald Heard, Christopher Isherwood,

Igor Stravinsky and his wife, and Eva Herrmann, an American artist and friend from their Sanary days.

Huxley was devastated, and wrote to several correspondents of his 'amputation'. He and Maria had been married for over thirty-five years, and she had devoted her life to him, eschewing a career, driving him around Europe and across America. They were of necessity more closely linked than most other couples; she had been his eyes. She had interpreted the world to him, and steered him through it. For several weeks Huxley stayed on in their house, throwing himself into work (on a dramatic version of his new novel), still accepting social invitations. Friends found him drawn and pale, openly talking of Maria, interested in ideas (to Isherwood's horror, discussing new developments in cancer research[4]), but lacking in warmth and intimacy. Once the play was complete, he prevailed upon a nervous Rose Nys (Maria's youngest sister) to drive him to New York in Maria's Oldsmobile; he would stay first in the playwright George Kaufman's Park Avenue flat (loving the unaccustomed luxury), and then with Matthew and his family in Connecticut. There he finished *Heaven and Hell*; once the books were out of the way, he embarked on a series of essays for *Esquire*, 'that curious magazine which combines naked girls, men's fashions and a certain amount of literature … Thanks to the nude ladies, they can pay very well.' He also learned that the medium Eileen Garrett had been in contact with Maria several times, and was able to get news of her via a New York medium (Garrett continued to pass on messages from Maria in the afterlife to Huxley at least until 1961[5]).

He returned to Los Angeles in October where he continued with his mescalin experiments, and also tried LSD. His essays for *Esquire* continued at $1,000 apiece, while a new collection, *Adonis and the Alphabet*, was assembled in early 1956. Then to everyone's surprise, the *Los Angeles Times* ran a headline, 'Novelist Huxley Weds Violinist'.

The violinist was Laura Archera, who had been a musical prodigy before becoming a psychotherapist. They had grown closer; some of his mescalin experiments had involved her, and, as she reported many years later, she began to identify with Maria. He had asked her whether she had ever been tempted by marriage (she was now forty-four, he sixty-one); she had replied that she had always wanted to protect her liberty as an independent woman. This did not seem to worry him; they headed off for the Drive-In Wedding Chapel in Arizona and married secretly in the presence of strangers as witnesses, an event, as he wrote to his friend Anita Loos, with distinctly comical aspects. However, the newspapers got hold of the story; Matthew in particular was offended that he had read about the marriage before his father had told him, while Maria's relatives seem to have been somewhat put out at his fickleness. Huxley had not been prepared for an enterprising journalist to claim the scoop before he had managed to break the news to family and friends, but given the bad feeling that followed the remarriage of his own father one might have expected him to be a little more considerate.

Once more Huxley moved house, to the Hollywood Hills. Laura kept her word about her independence, and spent much less time with Aldous. She was certainly less attentive to his needs and day-to-day help than Maria had been. She did not always accompany him on his travels, and often left him in California while she visited Europe. Huxley's Herculean efforts to put *The Genius and the Goddess* on Broadway came to very little; it closed after five nights in 1957, and led to rancour between the author and collaborator Beth Wendel on the one hand, and the director and producer on the other. By now Huxley had conquered his aversion to lecturing, and gave talks, television appearances and interviews frequently. He worked up some of his essays into an examination of psychological conditioning techniques, harking back to his best-known work with the title *Brave New World Revisited*. With that out of the way, he began work on what would prove to be his final completed novel, an ambitious attempt to create the utopian counterpart to his 1930s dystopia.

The second half of 1958 was taken up with a long voyage with Laura, at first to Peru, and then to Brazil as the honoured guest of the Brazilian government. Following this jaunt, which demonstrated his worldwide celebrity, they went to Italy and France, giving several lectures along the way. Aldous left Laura in Italy to visit England, where he made a couple of radio broadcasts, appearing with his brother Julian, the philosopher A.J. Ayer and the neurologist Grey Walter on *The Brains Trust*.[6]

The years 1959 and 1960 were spent lecturing at Santa Barbara,[7] Topeka, Berkeley, Dartmouth College, Pittsburgh, the Massachusetts Institute of Technology in Boston (where he held a Visiting Chair), Hawaii and elsewhere (he must have seen very little of Laura, who accompanied him only occasionally), and pushing on with the novel, *Island*. The genesis of the novel was difficult, and Huxley was painfully aware, as his letters to his publishers throughout this period make clear, of the unfavourable ratio of exposition to drama and lecturing to action. At one stage he tried to enlist Isherwood's help in improving the work. As it was, it turned out to be one of the longest novels he wrote – only *Point Counter Point* and *Eyeless in Gaza* were of comparable length.

He had problems organising and writing the novel. The material itself was difficult, and travelling and lecture-writing made concentration harder. There were personal problems too. Matthew's marriage ended, which saddened Aldous. Worse was the discovery of a cancerous growth on his tongue in May of 1960. Surgery was advised, but the removal of a large portion of his tongue would ruin his speech; not only did Huxley now get a large income from public speaking, but more to the point he had always been a great conversationalist. Instead, he opted for experimental treatment with radium needles. His doctor was amazed at Huxley's lack of concern for himself, and his objective interest in the science and medicine. The treatment was initially very successful, although friends and colleagues noticed that he was tired and pale.

In 1961, apart from a few more speaking engagements, Huxley was able to knuckle down to *Island*, but on 12 May, more disaster. A wildfire swept through southern California; Aldous and Laura were both in residence, and they managed to rescue a few precious items – the manuscript of *Island*, and Laura's Guarneri violin – before the flames reached the house. So much was lost – all of the letters between Aldous and Maria, many of Maria's letters to her family which had been returned to help Aldous who was contemplating an autobiography, Aldous's library complete with annotations, letters to Huxley from many distinguished correspondents, Lawrence's manuscript of *St Mawr* and T.H. Huxley's first edition of Voltaire's *Candide*. Huxley found himself a man without property, beginning a new life, bereft of his address books and diaries (he had made a lot of arrangements for the next few months, but had no idea where he was supposed to go when, or why). 'I am evidently intended to learn,' he wrote to a friend, 'a little in advance of the final denudation, that you can't take it with you.'

Despite these appalling blows, Huxley's schedule remained astonishing. Somehow (staying initially at Gerald Heard's house in Santa Monica) he finished the novel and went to England, leaving Laura in California, having avoided telling her about his latest worrying medical diagnosis. He stayed with Julian, and they visited Prior's Field together. He enjoyed the stage adaptation of *The Devils of Loudun*, before going off to Europe to stay with Maria's sister Jeanne, and then meeting Laura and Krishnamurti in Switzerland, where he paused to meet Albert Hofmann, the discoverer of LSD. Back in California in September, they took up residence in the house of a nearby friend who had fortunately been unaffected by the fire, but soon were off to India for the Tagore centenary celebrations, and then to San Francisco for a

Visiting Chair at Berkeley in early 1962, where he was rewarded with overflowing audiences for his lectures. After the publication of *Island*, his marathon continued with talks all around the US,[8] taking in Los Alamos where he lectured to the scientists and saw for himself the Apollo capsule, as well as the latest plane-to-ground missile technology. He complained to Osmond about the waste of money while so many were going hungry.

Island appeared in March 1962, the *summa* of Huxley's work, the positive message that he wished to leave to posterity. Though his health had not been of the best, Huxley does not seem to have expected or welcomed death, and indeed was in the early stages of another novel when he died; nevertheless, *Island is* precisely this kind of summation, a deliberately major novel – not since *Eyeless in Gaza* had Huxley put so much into a book. That this was Huxley's own view was confirmed by Laura Huxley in conversation reported by Nicholas Murray.[9] He knew it was not great literature; on the other hand, it is a book that demands to be taken seriously, especially when read in tandem with *Brave New World*. The reviews were mixed, generally poor (as ever for Huxley's later work), but most reviewers accepted that the work's literary qualities were secondary.

In June 1962, the cancer reappeared in his mouth and throat; there were minor treatments and operations, glands were removed. Its progress was slowed, but the rest of Huxley's life was spent under the shadow of illness and approaching death, as a guest in a borrowed house, very often away from his wife. He continued to work, lecture and travel, flying to Europe in August, staying with one of Maria's sisters in Amsterdam, and Julian in London, where he was delayed by a bout of influenza. Finally back in Los Angeles, he began his final book, *Literature and Science*, a fine intervention into the bad-tempered academic argument between British writers C.P. Snow and F.R. Leavis about the significance of the gap between the 'two cultures' – if anyone was able to bridge that gap, it would be Huxley. After that, he went back to

Europe in March 1963 for a conference and an audience with Pope John XXIII, and thence to New York to attend Matthew's second marriage, before lecturing once more in several places on the West Coast. Meanwhile, in the spring he began a new novel about the multiple levels upon which a person lives. It was to be an examination of a life, broadly based on Huxley's own, from all relevant standpoints simultaneously, showing how 'the universes we perceive and feel – one on each side of our skin – interweave and how they affect each other in an unending, interchanging circle'.[10]

It would have been incredible had Huxley's health stood the onslaught of work and travel; he was admitted to hospital for more radium treatment in May, but recovered enough to fly to Europe in August, attending a conference in Sweden, then staying with Julian in London, visiting many old friends, before joining Laura in Turin. The deterioration in his condition was very noticeable, commented upon by many, and his voice badly affected, first in volume and then, when an inflammation affected his vocal chords, in the range of his vocal abilities. He cancelled his scheduled lectures and, back in Los Angeles, finally let on to Julian and others about the cancer. He still refused to accept his own mortality; when Matthew and others visited him in the West, they had to pretend they were just passing through on business trips.

He worked until the end, first on a typewriter; then, when too weak for that, with pencil and paper; and when even weaker, speaking laboriously into a Dictaphone. His final work was an essay on 'Shakespeare and Religion', written at the cost of great physical and mental effort.[11] Nevertheless, it was as wide-ranging and closely argued as any of his fine cultural essays, a dying man's testimony of the duty to remain ethical in a hostile world, transforming and transfiguring it as Shakespeare's heroes tried, and often failed, to do. The whole process was extremely difficult, as Laura, typing the work as it developed, struggled with the unfamiliar Shakespearean words. The essay was finished to Aldous's satisfaction on 21 November.

On the 22nd, Aldous began to fail. He was put on oxygen; he asked for, and was given, LSD (twice – the first dose seemed to have no effect). Laura could not understand why the doctors were so interested in the television; only later did she learn of the assassination of President Kennedy. She held Aldous's hand, speaking the words from the *Tibetan Book of the Dead* that he had spoken to Maria eight years earlier. He lapsed into unconsciousness, and at 5.20 that afternoon died peacefully. He was cremated the next day, without ceremony.

In death as in life, Aldous Huxley was peripatetic; in 1971, his ashes were moved from their anonymous repository in California, and reburied – his final resting place – in his parents' grave at Compton, Surrey, where they were joined a year later by Maria's. Huxley's brother Trev already occupied the grave; Sir Julian, who died in 1975, and his wife Juliette, who died in 1994, were later buried with them. After a distinguished career as an anthropologist and epidemiologist, Matthew Huxley died in February 2005 at the age of eighty-four. Laura died in December 2007, at the age of ninety-six, still living in the borrowed house in the Hollywood Hills.

Work

The Doors of Perception (1954)

Huxley began his short book about his initial mescalin experiment within days, and it appeared in February 1954. The title was taken from William Blake's *Marriage of Heaven and Hell*:

> If the doors of perception were cleansed,
> Everything will appear to man as it is, infinite.

The piece contained his reflections on his experience, arguing for a connection between the psychedelic effect of mescalin and the mystical states, the value of which Huxley had been arguing for some time. The effect was as usual, dazzling – he was able for the first time in a long time to fuse his interests in science, religion, philosophy and art into an impressive fugue of debate.

Huxley was hoping for hallucinations and visions in the manner of De Quincey or Blake. Indeed, he often remarked on his failures in visualisation; when he wrote for the theatre his co-authors and adaptors were struck by his inability to 'see' the performance in his mind's eye. But although the drug did not improve his visual imagination, he felt that he was seeing a reality more 'real' than that mediated through the unaugmented senses. In one sequence, he looked at a flower arrangement; it was familiar, and he had remarked on it at breakfast that morning. But now, under the influence of the drug, he 'was seeing what Adam had seen on the morning of his creation – the miracle, moment by moment, of naked existence'. With Osmond, he experienced the world in his garden in Los Angeles, and then went for a short tour of the city. He was prompted to look at great works of art and ordinary objects; he listened to Mozart, Gesualdo and Berg. He opened the *Tibetan Book of the Dead* at random. He ate (he was not interested in food). They drove into the hills.

Interspersed with this *reportage*, he meditated about art (both European and Chinese), and music, and the relation between his own artificially induced perception and what he imagined visionary artists and mystics experienced. An interesting aside about the importance of drapery in painting followed thoughts he had already published in *Themes and Variations*, concluding that 'for the artist as for the mescalin taker, draperies are living hieroglyphs that stand in some peculiarly expressive way for the unfathomable mystery of pure being'. They provided opportunities for non-naturalistic interventions into otherwise representational contexts, and, as he had argued in the earlier piece, this enabled the artist to suggest his own idea of the relationship between perception and reality.

He linked his new experiences to the metaphysical scheme of *The Perennial Philosophy* that God and mind are in everything. Because objects seemed isolated and denuded of their usual associations, it was like seeing the world anew. Nothing needed to be special to impress him; the weave of the flannel in his trousers fascinated him. He felt decentred; no longer was his self the fulcrum of his experience. He described how the distinctions between inner and outer, between self and world, between him and other, broke down. He felt a sense of union, unsurprisingly hard to describe, with a garden chair.

At the end of this short book, he added a coda arguing that mescalin is socially useful, that more should be known about it and that it should be easily available, because 'the urge to transcend self-conscious selfhood is … a principal appetite of the soul'. He backed up this claim with statistics and references to the available psychological, theological and biochemical research, and pointed to the persistent popularity in all societies of methods to transcend humdrum daily life, ranging from art, religion, carnivals, dancing and oratory, as well as chemical intoxicants legal and illegal. The coda is not convincing; the reader may feel that these activities are evidence less of the primeval urge to transcend selfhood, than of the unsatisfactoriness of daily life.

The Genius and the Goddess (1955)

Huxley's titles were usually masterpieces of allusion. He seems to have had problems with that of his penultimate novel, whose original title was *Through the Wrong End of the Opera Glasses*, referring to the distance with which one views one's past. His second effort was a misquote from *The Tempest*, *The Past is Prelude*, but a member of his American publisher Harper's staff coined *The Genius and the Goddess*, which Huxley liked as

'straightforward, appealing and [having] good precedents, like
The Virgin and the Gypsy'.[12]

This was Huxley's slightest novel in both length and sub-
stance, although the writing and adaptation to the theatre cost
him great efforts. Yet in it he solved, possibly for the only time,
the problem he had in portraying saints. Sinners, he could do –
Mond, Obispo, Mrs Thwale were all magnificent characters – but
he struggled with the Propters, Millers and Rontinis who shoul-
dered the burden of his positive message. In *The Genius and the
Goddess*, he used the Conradian device of embedded narratives;
the anonymous narrator narrates John Rivers's narration about
well-known physicist Henry Maartens and his beautiful wife
Katy. Rivers tells us in his own words what lessons he learned
from his youthful affair with Katy, while the extra narrator lends
helpful distance.

The story is a conventional morality tale: Katy seduces Rivers,
who is also loved by her daughter Ruth. They fight over him, and
are killed together, with the usual Huxleian grotesquerie: Katy's
beautiful face is destroyed, 'rubbed out on the bloody macadam
of the road'. Maartens does not care – a genius yes, but an idiot
savant, an incomplete man reminiscent of *Antic Hay*'s Shearwater,
his knowledge divorced from the practical realities of life – and
he quickly and happily remarries. Rivers is devastated.

The real message of the story appears at the beginning.
The narrator and Rivers have a connection; the narrator once
unsuccessfully proposed to Helen, who later, after the death of
Katy, married Rivers and saved him from a life of despair. Helen
is now dead, but remains a key presence in the novel. As Rivers
puts it:

> Dying's an art, and at our age we ought to be learning it. It helps
> to have seen someone who really knew how. Helen knew how
> to die because she knew how to live – how to live now and here
> and for the greater glory of God.

The earlier quadrangle in which Rivers had become entangled could only produce unhappiness; Helen saved Rivers from a wasted life.

It is hard not to read autobiographical commentary into *The Genius and the Goddess*; it was the last book of Huxley's that Maria read, and one that she loved, and by the time it was published, she, like Helen, was dead. Is the title gesturing obliquely towards the geniuses and goddesses with whom Huxley passed his time before he met Maria? Might there be a reference to the seductive but empty charms of life at Garsington? In *Time Must Have a Stop*, Eustace Barnack, even after death, could not forsake the sensual delights of this world for enlightenment. In contrast, we are sure that Rivers will welcome the annihilation of the self.

Heaven and Hell (1956)

Like *The Doors of Perception*, the title *Heaven and Hell* was taken from Blake, appropriately enough since it was intended as a sequel (the two short essays are usually published together in a single volume). However, the two works are different in tone – *Heaven and Hell* hardly mentions psychedelic drugs at all. Whereas *The Doors of Perception* centred on the altered consciousness of the author considered introspectively, *Heaven and Hell* was a study of the means by which consciousness has been altered, particularly by art, across cultures and civilisations. It was therefore a universalisation of Huxley's mescalin-based experiences; its premise was that mescalin enables the user to explore hitherto unknown regions of his own mind, exactly as other types of experience, including those induced by ritual, art and mystical visions.

Huxley argued that those who alter their consciousness explore the antipodes of their experience and find weird and wonderful marsupials there. *Heaven and Hell* was a bestiary of the antipodes, with a series of methods for reaching it – hypnosis, dreams, visions, the use of precious stones and other brightly coloured materials, jewellery, glass and gold, art and ritual. A series of appendices, mini-essays on topics such as how poor diet aids mystic experience, the rarity of close-up landscapes in Western art and the demonic work of Géricault, rounded off the piece.

As an account of the antipodes of the mind, this wasn't particularly convincing. Supposed commonalities across cultures were postulated – for instance, 'praeternatural light and colour are common to all visionary experiences ... along with ... a recognition of heightened significance'; 'Most paradises are adorned with buildings, and, like the trees, the waters, the hills and fields, these buildings are bright with gems.' Huxley took the existence of these commonalities, some of which are tendentious in the extreme, to mean that they faithfully reflect and express visionary human experience. Once more, his scepticism failed him entirely when he was judging mystic or visionary discourse.

As a philosophical or psychological argument, *Heaven and Hell* was unsatisfactory, yet it contained some characteristically impressive analyses of art, and of how the conditions of human life alter our conceptions of the world, whether human, natural or supernatural. Appendix III was a highlight, a short narrative history of pyrotechnics and illumination in the context of popular entertainment, showing the complacent mid-twentieth-century reader how magical these effects would seem in a world where night was often lit by a single candle.

Adonis and the Alphabet/Tomorrow and Tomorrow and Tomorrow (1956)

The American title of this collection, *Tomorrow and Tomorrow and Tomorrow*, was from Macbeth's wonderful soliloquy (from which *Brief Candles* was also taken) of nihilism and lack of hope, where life 'is a tale told by an idiot, full of sound and fury, signifying nothing' (the title of the English edition is taken from one of the essays). Of the eighteen pieces, six appeared for the first time on publication in late 1956; most of the others were from Huxley's *Esquire* column in 1955–6, while the earliest had appeared, like many of Huxley's pieces at this time, in *Vedanta and the West*, the official journal of the Vedanta Society of southern California, which at one stage had been edited by Isherwood, and upon whose editorial board Huxley himself sat.

The collection was structured around a pair of major pieces, 'The Education of an Amphibian' and 'Knowledge and Understanding', which explored the relevance of his mystical ideas for our psychological life – in particular the contrast between factual knowledge in terms of concepts describing reality, and a deep understanding or direct awareness of reality. This distinction was the starting point for a series of thoughts about idealisations of and improvements to the world we live in, using the metaphor of amphibiousness as a new and somewhat more positive term for the 'wearisome condition':

> Simultaneously or alternately, we inhabit many different and even incommensurable universes … [W]e are simultaneously the subjects of Nature and the citizens of a strictly human republic, which may be anything from what St Paul called 'no mean city' to the most squalid of material and moral slums … I shall talk about the troubles of an ape that has learned to talk – of an immortal spirit that has not yet learned to dispense with words.
>
> ('The Education of an Amphibian')

In 'Ozymandias' he examined the failure of a cooperative community at Llano del Rio near Los Angeles, while 'Domesticating Sex' looked at nineteenth-century experiments in communal free love. In the extraordinary 'Hyperion to a Satyr', an extended meditation on sanitation morphed into a discussion of purity, via his theory of the incompleteness of words/concepts as descriptions of subtle reality. Cleaning up Britain's slums, symbols of lower-class deprivation, may be a good thing, but:

> this does not guarantee us against the creation of new symbols no less compulsive in their anti-democratic tendencies than the old. A man may be clean; but if, in a dictatorship, he lacks a party card, he figuratively stinks.

In 'Mother', Huxley's musings about Hallmark cards' schmaltz ('in the paradise of commercialised maternity, no Freudian reptile, it is evident, has ever reared its ugly head') were enlivened by digressions on the torments of Job and the Hindu mother Kali as destroyer. American popular culture, the Cold War, the persistent misunderstanding of the nature of the human mind and the neglect of the human spiritual dimension are consistent themes of the collection.

Brave New World Revisited (1958)

This non-fiction work, adapted from a series of articles in the American newspaper *Newsday* collectively called 'Tyranny over the Mind', appeared in October 1958. Huxley conceived and wrote it after he had already begun *Island*; rethinking and reshaping of the tropes of *Brave New World* had led him to investigate and muse upon the state of the art in the technology of mind control and covert oppression. Furthermore, he may also have been spurred into action by the success of Vance Packard's *The Hidden Persuaders*,[13] a bestselling exposé of the motivational research and subliminal psychology underlying the advertising industry, which he had read in 1957. The resulting piece was hardly a major work in its own right, and of course is now outdated, but it was thought-provoking enough as a commentary on the potential for oppression in the twentieth-century democracies during the Cold War. Huxley was not concerned with weaponry or torture; as usual, he was interested in the individual. What is the condition of freedom in an age of overpopulation, environmental degradation and technology? Where does autonomy begin?

He reminded the reader that *Brave New World* was written in 1931, and set several centuries into the future. In 1958, he now felt that the technologies postulated in the earlier book were reaching maturity, at a time when 'freedom and even the desire for this freedom seems to be on the wane'. He contrasted his particular brand of pessimism with Orwell's; *Nineteen Eighty-Four*, he opined, was a brilliant portrayal of the possibilities of totalitarianism that were undreamt of in 1931, but he maintained that the technology of reinforcing 'desirable' behaviour through rewards was a more efficient, and therefore greater, threat to freedom than that symbolised by Orwell's image of 'a boot stamping on a human face – forever'. He may also have been piqued by the frequent parallels drawn in *The Hidden Persuaders* between the ad-men's power over consumers and the Orwellian world of *Nineteen Eighty-Four*, while Packard ignored *Brave New World* as a cultural reference point altogether; Packard himself gets only a passing mention in *Brave New World Revisited*.

The essays set out the dilemmas. The world was overpopulated and human progress, particularly medical advances, were cutting down the number of premature deaths. Huxley's interest in eugenics was still evident in his worry that IQ was decreasing, and that the less intelligent were breeding faster. The numbers did not add up; the pressures on resources, and the likely decrease in the ability of rational argument to hold sway, already posed a powerful and unprecedented threat to freedom. Added to that was the scientific/technological imperative to reduce multiplicity, to simplify and thereby dehumanise society, which had centralised government and decreased the capacity of communities to govern themselves in the Kropotkinesque way Huxley had championed since the 1930s. Low IQs combined with more education created opportunities for propaganda via the mass media. Yet political theory was powerless to understand this new force; the dark arts of persuasion were now devoted to the banal task of selling things. Yet there were also more dangerous and aggressive methods, including brainwashing, chemical persuasion, subliminal persuasion and hypnotherapy, to contend with. Huxley's solutions – educate about propaganda, facilitate birth control, distribute property fairly, decentralise and deurbanise society – seem somewhat lame in the light of the terrifying and implacable processes he described in the rest of the work.

Island (1962)

Island, unsuccessful in many ways, a critical failure, containing more sanctimony than inspiration, is nevertheless an important work in the Huxley canon, the best piece of fiction since *Time Must Have a Stop*, and Huxley's most significant novel since *Eyeless in Gaza*. It was his utopia, a synthesis of his recent thinking, a final attempt to move beyond the pessimism that had driven his most sincere writing throughout his career, and a deliberate reuse and revaluation of the conceptual framework of *Brave New World*, weaving its themes into his utopia, positive images, as it were, of the dystopian negatives. The short title (Huxley was particularly pleased with the Danish title – a 'miracle of brevity' – Ø) alluded in a sideways way to his dystopia, whose title referred to the invasion of Prospero's island by imperfect beings from the outer world. It is set on an island of sanity, a point of good sense and fine, rational behaviour in an irrational and venal world. Quite clearly it describes the third alternative to insanity and primitivism that he proposed in his 1946 Foreword to *Brave New World*.

The island of Pala is a hidden world governed by the perennial philosophy. Everything is intended to save its population from sorrow. The trees are full of mynah birds trained to squawk 'Attention!' and 'Here and now!' to remind people to concentrate on their present being in the world, and not to dwell on past horrors. A journalist, Will Farnaby, is shipwrecked; he carries no baggage except characteristically Huxleian guilt at his ill treatment of his deceased wife and his alienating sexual relations with his promiscuous mistress. He is in a state of shock, yet a little girl from the island gently brings him back to the present, forcing him to relive his traumas until he has escaped their grip.

This is the beginning of a remarkable adventure for Will, who is introduced to the society of Pala where Huxley's ideals have been implemented. Pain and suffering are inevitable, but desire and fear are, as far as possible, eliminated through training, practice and concentration. Psychological rationality is a deliberate aim of the society. Western technology is used where it is felt necessary, but the technological tail does not wag the social dog; Eastern mysticism determines the limits to which it is needed. Birth control is practised, sex is guilt-free and not covert, and the family unit is deliberately diluted to socialise children. Death is faced stoically; one character, a much-loved wife, dies in a dignified way in a scene echoing the death of Maria. The population uses moksha, a psychedelic drug that gives them the sort of perceptive insight that Huxley described in *The Doors of Perception*, but it is taken only sparingly in public ceremonies, not for recreational use.

It is a doomed Eden. The neighbouring state, a 'normal' nation, needs Pala's oil supply, and Pala's Crown Prince Murugan betrays his nation with Will's unwitting connivance. The soldiers invade, and paradise is lost.

Huxley, in writing *Island*, was rethinking *Brave New World*. The appearance of *Brave New World Revisited* while he was writing the novel already suggests that he was trying to understand his older critique in a modern context. He reworked a number of institutions from *Brave New World* to build *Island*'s higher utilitarianism. Most obviously there was the drug *moksha* for transcendental perception, as opposed to *soma*'s use to create a quiescent population. Both societies used hypnotic and sub-liminal learning techniques, but in the earlier book this was for the purposes of indoctrination. In both books families were deemed artificial and inappropriate for rational child-rearing, sex was guilt-free and reproduction managed with technology. In *Island* this was to distribute the risk that children would be adversely affected by the neuroses of a single set of parents, while in *Brave New World* the idea was to diminish individuality.

This was a tricky act for Huxley to pull off, as there was a danger that the criticisms one might apply to the *Brave New World* dystopia might just as easily apply to Pala. Huxley urged us to look at the whole picture; individuality in Pala *was* restricted, but only to prevent the individual's autonomy affecting the rationality of the society as a whole. Fostering genuine psycho-logical well-being was admittedly similar to the dystopian prac-tice of creating the *simulacrum* of well-being via the manipulation of the population's preferences. Ultimately, the success of Huxley's project – which thus stated was impressively audacious, whether or not he succeeded – rested on the argument from *Ends and Means* that doing good depends on being good. *Island* encapsu-lated Huxley's concerns because he took the daring route of reusing the components of *Brave New World*; the contrast afforded was so much more instructive because the Palans shared many attitudes and assumptions with Mustapha Mond's cohorts.

Literature and Science (1963)

It is hard to look at the output of Huxley's final few years, in the full awareness of hindsight, without seeing it in a valedictory light. *Brave New World Revisited*, as the title suggested, updated the science behind his greatest work, while *Island* revisited the argu-ments and tried to put a positive case for progress. Huxley's final book appropriately explored the territory where he spent all of his life, where literature and science collide. This man was immersed in the two cultures – he was amply qualified to comment on a brief but fiery spat between two of Britain's pre-eminent intellectuals, C.P. Snow and F.R. Leavis.

Snow was a well-known novelist – his semi-autobiographical sequence *Strangers and Brothers* has not stood the test of time *qua* literature (though at least one of the novels, *The Masters*, deserves resurrection), but it is an invaluable evocation of the potent mix of science, defence and politics in the 1950s – and also had careers as a physicist, a senior civil servant, and a politician. In the Rede Lecture at Cambridge on the topic of 'The Two Cultures and the Scientific Revolution', he had argued forcefully that there was a 'gulf of mutual incomprehension' between scientists and literary intellectuals. Writers had no idea what simple terms like 'mass' or 'acceleration' meant, or what the second law of thermodynamics entailed; on the other hand, scientists had no acquaintance with important literary works. Snow went to on link this mutual incomprehension with many of the problems of the day which could be open to scientific solution, and to argue that science was vital to secure civilisation's future. However, the British education system overvalued the humanities, such as Latin and Greek, and correspondingly restricted access to useful scientific education. Snow was answered by Leavis, an outspoken Cambridge English don who used his Richmond Lecture to rip into his opponent with a vengeance. Snow was a 'public relations man' for science, who is 'utterly without a glimmer of what creative literature is, and why it matters', and 'is intellectually as undistinguished as it is possible to be'.

Huxley was disgusted by this argument, and charted a middle road between Snow's 'bland scientism' and the 'violent and ill-mannered' Leavis's 'one-track, moralistic literarism' by examining the role, function and psychology of literature and science, and thinking about their past, present and potential relationships.

Each had its own purpose and assumptions. Each tried to purify the 'words of the tribe' (our common language, a phrase taken from Mallarmé's *The Tomb of Edgar Allen Poe*); science tried to reduce ambiguities, while literature tried to deepen meaning via various means including metaphor and imagery. The result was that an object like a nightingale could have very different descriptions depending on whether one was being poetical or biological. In a scientific age a creative writer would be making a mistake if he denied the significance of scientific description, while the scientist who ignored the literary would lose sight of the significance of the things he studied.

Literature and Science appeared in September 1963; by the end of November, Aldous Huxley was dead.

Thought

From the early satires to the later jeremiads, Huxley had lacked a practical positive vision. This was not for want of trying, but neither his flirtation with Lawrentian ideas, nor his work with the Peace Pledge Union, nor his researches into Eastern philosophy provided a practical route to whatever was necessary to save the world from itself.

Consequently, although most commentators view the early 1930s when Huxley was wrestling with *Eyeless in Gaza* as the major discontinuity in the Huxleian canon, *The Doors of Perception* marked a much more radical development.[14] The mystical Huxley failed to challenge the ironist and the pessimist, but his realisation that the mystical states which he so admired were attainable via straightforward chemical means gave his philosophy a new practical and positive aspect. He began to mention 'the world's fundamental all-rightness'; his disgust for physicality seemed to disappear; death ceased to be a scourge; communication between humans, almost non-existent in his previous novels, now became possible; alienation was no longer the default. Mescalin brought his mystical view of reality into the realm of science and technology.

Mescalin and mysticism

Huxley's experiment confirmed for him a philosophical hypothesis derived from Henri Bergson and C.D. Broad that perception is an eliminative faculty. The brain is bombarded with information via the sense organs, and its job is to filter out as much as possible to prevent the mind being overwhelmed by sensation (physiologically, that is more or less what happens). When the doors of perception are cleansed, we see more of reality than we otherwise would. The brain's filter is extremely important, as ordinary life would be impossible without it (Huxley describes a rising terror that takes hold of him at one point in *The Doors of Perception*). However, under the influence of mescalin, Huxley found something more; was this not evidence of God-in-the-world?

The alteration of the mind had become irrevocably technological. Huxley was not neglectful of the essentially chemical and artificial nature of the psychological changes he experienced. Naturally the view he achieved under the influence of the drug was strange and unusual; he had deliberately altered the conditions under which his brain was to operate. Yet did this not suggest that the mystic experiences that had impressed him so much in *The Perennial Philosophy* could have similar causes?

Huxley was the last person to shy away from this conclusion, and indeed welcomed it, as evidence that (a) mystical experiences were not restricted to a special, intuitive type of person, and (b) they were not essentially mysterious. Methods of alteration of the mind may well have often rested on alteration, even abuse, of the body (in *The Perennial Philosophy* Huxley had discussed mortification), and he argued in *Heaven and Hell* that 'most contemplatives worked systematically to modify their body chemistry with a view to creating the internal conditions favourable to spiritual insight'. The Huxleian exploration of the wearisome condition showed that one should not deny the profundity or importance of a thought just because it could be shown to have had a physical or chemical cause in the body.

Furthermore, he did not usually make the error of thinking that mescalin was a route to the same enlightened thinking that he believed the mystics experienced. The mescalin experience was what theologians call a 'gratuitous grace' – an unmerited gift from God which arrives despite the recipient's being in a state of mortal sin, and which is neither sufficient, nor necessary, for salvation. Drugs will not give the user a Beatific Vision, though, if used wisely, may help him on his way and make the nature of the world, and God in the world, clearer. As a consequence of his disdain for organised religion, he was happy to hint that the altered conception of reality obtained via mescalin is more help to the aspiring seeker of truth than the rituals and observances of a mainstream church. However that may be, at the minimum they allow the user to see the world in a different way, which means that he can challenge the quotidian reality with which he is usually confronted.

However, in *Heaven and Hell*, Huxley did admittedly go further and unwisely stressed the similarities between the experiences of a mescalin user and those of the mystic visionaries. He was already on weak ground having accepted mystics' introspective visions as veridical, and the significance of their similarity with psychedelic experiences needed far more evidence to establish. Indeed, in *The Doors of Perception*, Huxley also pointed out similarities between the mental states of mescalin users and schizophrenics; clearly, similarity to other modes of thought was no basis for a serious argument about the positive merits of mescalin use.

The 'unimaginably subtle' world

Huxley also applied this analysis of perception to the relation between thought, language and the world, extending his earlier critique of ideology. He was now able to connect the crudity of language with the relatively impoverished awareness that humans typically have of the world. In the context of the hyperawareness to which Huxley believed he had access, it is unsurprising that linguistic tradition should 'bedevil [a person's] sense of reality' – a view influenced by the linguist Benjamin Lee Whorf, whose work Huxley was reading in 1952. It also explained why people were unaware of what Huxley now called Mind at Large – the languages we speak, evolved for communication, not accurate description of reality, mean that we have only partial and imperfect contact with this Greater Mind.

Language remained an important preoccupation for Huxley right up to the last paragraph of his final book, *Literature and Science*:

> Thought is crude, matter unimaginably subtle. Words are few and can only be arranged in certain conventionally fixed ways; the counterpoint of unique events is infinitely wide and their succession indefinitely long. That the purified language of science, or even the richer purified language of literature should ever be adequate to the givenness of the world and of our experience is, in the very nature of things, impossible. Cheerfully accepting the fact, let us advance together, men of letters and men of science, further and further into the ever expanding regions of the unknown.

In 'The Education of an Amphibian' from *Adonis and the Alphabet*, he argued that 'every existing language is an implied theory of man and his universe, a virtual philosophy'. Names imply things. He went on, in the title essay, to argue that 'the internal realm of concepts … corresponds to the external realm of perceived "forms" … [N]o language is perfect, no vocabulary adequate to the wealth of the given universe'. Hence the forms we perceive, determined by the words we have access to via our languages and cultures, cannot be the whole 'togetherness of all things in an endless hierarchy of living and interacting patterns'.

This led to Huxley making a distinction (in many of the essays in *Adonis and the Alphabet*, but see especially 'Knowledge and Understanding') between 'knowledge', a grasp of ideas bolstered by memory and analytic reasoning, 'always in terms of concepts [which] can be passed on by means of words or other symbols', and 'understanding', 'direct awareness of the raw material' of experience, which 'is not conceptual, and therefore cannot be passed on'. We increase our knowledge when 'we succeed in fitting a new experience into the system of concepts based on our old experiences'. On the other hand, 'understanding comes when we liberate ourselves from the old and so make possible a direct, unmediated contact with the new, the mystery, moment by moment, of our existence'. Knowledge is needed for understanding, but understanding must transcend knowledge. The danger is that the two will be confused – that someone armed with mere knowledge would think they understood the world, and mistake the mystery for the term that denoted it, or, worse, think that by naming a problem they had thereby solved it. The invention of the alphabet was our greatest, and yet most dangerous, discovery. As he argued in 'Hyperion to a Satyr' from *Adonis and the Alphabet*:

> symbols are necessary – for we could not live without them. But they are also fatal – for the thinking they make possible is just as often unrealistic as it is to the point. In this consists the essentially tragic nature of the human situation.

Final thoughts on education

Can anything be done about this? In *Island*, Huxley gave us his final thoughts on education as an under-secretary shows Will Farnaby around a Palanese school. The ideas of *Brave New World* were put into a positive context and transformed, although not all readers will be convinced. The under-secretary contrasts the purpose of education in Pala with that in the rest of the world. In Russia and China, children are manufactured to serve the state. In the democracies:

> what are boys and girls for …? Answer: for mass consumption. And the corollaries of mass consumption are mass communications, mass advertising, mass opiates in the form of television, meprobamate, positive thinking and cigarettes.

Meprobramate was an early blockbuster tranquilising drug in the United States, withdrawn in 1970 when its addictive nature became clear. Ironically, a variant of meprobamate, carisoprodol, was marketed under the name *Soma*.

In contrast, the education of Palanese children is for 'actualization, for being turned into full-blown human beings'. They are classified early on into psychological types: sheep-people (gregarious people, hence viscerotonics), cat-people (loners, hence cerebrotonics) and marten-people (doers, hence somatotonics).

> What we give the children is simultaneously a training in perceiving and imagining … applied physiology and psychology … practical ethics and practical religion … the proper use of language, and … self-knowledge. In a word, a training of the whole mind-body in all its aspects.

Through the mouth of the under-secretary, Huxley summed up his philosophy of education, deploring the teaching of facts and abstractions, preferring the adaptation of the child to the complexities of the world with which he or she could live in harmony.

This followed a deeper exploration of education in 'The Education of an Amphibian' (and also 'Knowledge and Understanding'). Traditional education, based on the seven liberal arts, was always verbal and therefore focused on knowledge, not understanding. Huxley urged that education be aimed more towards the non-verbal understanding, to enable us to function as properly immersed, non-conflicted amphibians, to 'educate the [whole] psycho-physical instrument'. To that end, he suggested a five-level curriculum.

The first was training of the kinaesthetic sense, sometimes called 'proprioception', which perceives the relative positions of parts of the body (Huxley no doubt preferred the former term with its implication of active movement to the latter implying passive reception of sense data). This followed from his preoccupation with the link between the mind and quite rudimentary, routine and basic states of the body; how can we think good thoughts if our bodies are functioning inefficiently and incorrectly? We must unlearn poor habits of stance, posture and movement, and restore correctness to our use of our bodies. To do this, Huxley prescribed the Alexander Technique, quoting John Dewey to the effect that 'it bears the same relation to education that education itself bears to all other human activities'.

The second level was training of the five senses, and the third was training of memory. In each case Huxley cited the work of Gestalt psychologist Samuel Renshaw whose work became well known in the 1940s and 1950s when he was able to improve people's perception. Ordinary undergraduates developed palettes as finely attuned as whiskey blenders', while American troops learned to identify enemy planes quickly and accurately. According to Huxley, Renshaw's 'psychological optics' were derived from the pioneering ideas of Bates. The fourth level was training to control the automatic nervous system, with techniques of relaxation, auto-suggestion and post-hypnotic suggestion. Finally, the fifth level was training in the art of spiritual insight, akin to, but very different from, psychoanalysis:

> The aim of the psychiatrist is to teach the (statistically) abnormal to adjust themselves to the behaviour patterns of a society composed of the (statistically) normal. The aim of the educator in spiritual insight is to teach the (statistically) normal that they are in fact insane and should do something about it.

Huxley used ideas from Zen Buddhism and Krishnamurti about freeing thought and perception from the concepts and unanalysed postulates 'in terms of which we do our second-hand experiencing'.

Is such a curriculum desirable, he asked himself (rhetorically). Unsurprisingly 'my answer is an emphatic yes'. But to the question of its practicability he was oddly equivocal. Indeed, he seemed to advocate kicking the issue into the long grass:

> What is needed at the present stage is research-intensive, extensive and long-drawn research. Some Foundation with a few scores of millions to get rid of should finance a ten- or fifteen-year plan of observation and experiment. At the end of this period, we should know which are the most important items in a programme of psychophysical training, how they can best be taught in primary schools, secondary schools, and colleges, and what benefits may be expected to follow such a course of training.

After the years of thinking on educational matters that Huxley had already put in, it seems somewhat pusillanimous for him then to ask, somewhat diffidently, for a long-term research programme. No doubt research would be needed to get the system adopted in all or most schools in the Western world, but there seems little reason why someone should not simply start a school and begin teaching. Huxley retained his admiration for expertise and professionalism even as he chafed at the failures of imagination of experts and educationalists.

Education or conditioning?

Huxley's disdain for the common man and his uninteresting pursuits still handicapped his thinking. He defended the importance of the individual against thinkers such as Herbert Spencer and B.F. Skinner who claimed that all apparent individuality is 'really' down to environmental factors. But Huxley only ever rebutted that view with an example of a great or heroic individual, usually Shakespeare. For ordinary individuals he had less time, and for them Huxleian education looked very like propaganda.

For instance, after a blood-curdling sequence of chapters about propaganda in *Brave New World Revisited*, he concluded that society really *needs* propaganda to function. The Institute of Propaganda Analysis was founded in 1937 to combat the Nazis, and was disbanded in 1941 when the Allied governments discovered that they could gain from psychological warfare too. Anti-rationalist propagandists deform and misuse language, so people should be taught how this is done and how to combat it, and people should be taught about the techniques for mind control that they are likely to encounter from the mass media. But mind control is not always a bad thing; in *Heaven and Hell* he argued that:

> the gorgeous fancy dress worn by Kings, Popes and their respective retainers, military and ecclesiastical, has a very practical purpose – to impress the lower classes with a lively sense of their masters' superhuman greatness.

And in *Brave New World Revisited* he wrote that:

> Too searching a scrutiny by too many of the common folk of
> what is said by their pastors and masters might prove to be pro-
> foundly subversive. In its present form, the social order depends
> on its continued existence on the acceptance, without too many
> embarrassing questions, of the propaganda put forth by those in
> authority and the propaganda hallowed by the local traditions.
> The problem, once more, is to find the happy mean. Individuals
> must be suggestible enough to be willing and able to make their
> society work, but not so suggestible as to fall helplessly under
> the spell of professional mind-manipulators.

He suggested judging propaganda with regard to how it fitted in
with three overriding values: individual freedom, based on diversity and the genetic uniqueness of each individual; the promotion
of love and compassion; and intelligence.

Is this an example of irony? Note the qualification: the proposition is about society 'in its present form'. Huxley was not in
favour of over-centralised, over-mechanised civilisation. Perhaps
this paragraph was a sly dig at the hypocrisy of a democrat who
did not challenge the status quo. Such a person, however well
intentioned, would be subtly reliant on the same techniques, in
religion, in the forces, in the advertising industry that supports
capitalism, in politics, to ensure popular thought was predictable
and well understood.

Huxley's philosophy of means and ends illuminates matters.
In *The Perennial Philosophy* he made the point that advertising is
a bad thing not just because it leads to inauthenticity in people's
lives, nor because it is a distraction from concentration and meditation ('unrestrained and indiscriminate talk is morally evil and
spiritually dangerous', he says in the chapter on 'Silence'). Most
importantly, advertising's function is to create and increase craving, desire, dissatisfaction. But deliverance and enlightenment can

only take place in a state of desirelessness. What is bad about the advertiser's attempt to alter minds is not the mind-altering so much as the constant babble of the battle for one's explicit attention, and the advertisement's evil purpose of increasing desire.

To be honest, it is not clear how ironic is the quoted passage about propaganda; Huxley did not approve of modern society, but nor did he approve of modern people. He was a decentralising anarchist who was at the same time an elitist and at his worst something of a snob. Many of his characters held the same equivocal attitudes; Walter Bidlake in *Point Counter Point* 'wished that he could personally like the oppressed and personally hate the rich oppressors', while 'the proximity of the poor always made [Sebastian Barnack from *Time Must Have a Stop*] feel uncomfortable'. Huxley had little or no idea of the mechanisms and structures that govern human behaviour, especially in advanced societies. He often combined brilliant identification, analysis and diagnosis of problems with inadequate and unnecessarily draconian solutions.

How to do good

The reader of Huxley's later works cannot help but remark on the difficulties of doing good. Since *Ends and Means* and *Eyeless in Gaza*, he had insisted that to *do* good, one had to *be* good. One could not, *contra* Bentham and the utilitarians, produce good effects by doing harm. This uncompromising opposition to fashionable consequentialism was one of Huxley's most important claims, but his works often perversely ended up showing the impossibility of doing much good at all. Propter in *After Many a Summer* appeared to do little, although he theorised at great length; in *Time Must Have a Stop*, Rontini's efforts had precious little effect on the Barnacks until his death. Huxley himself had lectured, been to conferences and made proposals, but his political programme was a long way short of being implemented. But from *The Doors of Perception* onward, Huxley argued more explicitly that because cerebrotonic contemplatives' virtues were negative, positive goodness was needed instead.

In *The Doors of Perception*, Huxley did not try to solve the problem, but progress was made merely by expressing it. 'How could one reconcile this timeless bliss of seeing as one ought to see with the temporal duties of doing what one ought to do and feeling as one ought to feel?' He sensed a contradiction that lingered over his work. He explored and eventually propounded mysticism as a response to the problem of evil in the world, specifically the build-up in military tension in the 1930s, yet mysticism is not fundamentally a moral philosophy. It may be that all mystics are good, and Huxley at various places seemed to argue that they are, but this appears to be accidentally true at best, and it is based on a rarefied metaphysical view of 'good' that has very little to do with being good in the world and doing good to one's fellow man. In *The Perennial Philosophy*, he had argued explicitly that 'good is the separate self's conformity to, and finally annihilation in, the divine Ground which gives it being; evil, the intensification of separateness, the refusal to know that the Ground exists'. Any link to other people, or the consequences of one's actions, is purely coincidental. For Huxley, *The Doors of Perception* seemed to smooth the way to a more involved philosophy, connected to one's fellow man and the world, able, willing and desiring to do good in the world, like the Bodhisattvas of the admired Mahayana Buddhist tradition.

By emphasising inclusion and sociability, Huxley's art had finally caught up with his oft-preached injunction to live in the world and inside the Godhead simultaneously, to live everywhere one can. The wise mystics of Huxley's middle years, Miller, Propter and Rontini, were older men, remote from the world, without family. For the first time, *Island* brought us mystical teachers embedded in the world, young as well as old, women as well as men, functioning with families and friends. The place for the mystic teacher was within society, not aloof from it. Indeed, the first bit of wisdom that Will Farnaby was given in *Island* came from a little girl, Mary Sarojini (unless we count the slogans of the mynah birds with which the novel opens). He made his most effective statements of this inclusive creed in the last piece he wrote, 'Shakespeare and Religion':

> We must not live thoughtlessly, taking our illusion for the complete reality, but at the same time we must not live too thoughtfully in the sense of trying to escape from the dream state. We must continually be on our watch for ways in which we may enlarge our consciousness. We must not attempt to live outside the world, which is given us, but we must somehow learn to transform it and transfigure it.

The giant figure of Shakespeare, whose understanding of the world of physics and pratfalls, and the parallel world of spirit and poetry, was in each case unsurpassed, is entirely appropriate as a prompt for such thoughts.

Sex and love

At the same time, the late works of Huxley began to resolve the problems of love and sex which had been another of his staple topics. Since the early satires, he had become increasingly sardonic, reaching a nadir with the repulsive sexual content of *Ape and Essence*. He had, as usual, based his ideas on the work of a now-forgotten scientist, in this case one J.D. Unwin, for whom he wrote a Foreword, and whom he discussed in *Ends and Means*. Unwin had suggested that sex presents us with a binary choice: abstain and be continent, energetic and useful, or indulge and be permanently tired and useless. The problem, as Huxley saw it, was that those, like the Puritans, who sublimated their sexual urges were often more dangerous than useful, so it was important to ensure that the energy released by chastity was channelled in 'ethically reputable' ways.

In his last two novels, Huxley finally wrote about sex as less of a problem, more of a solution, and in *Island* the irritatingly perfect Palanese were able to sustain fulfilling and happy relationships. Even so, the detail is beyond our reach, and happiness is transitory. Dr MacPhail's wife dies of cancer. Susila's husband has died in an accident. It is merely stated that the Vijayas are happy; neither what that happiness consists in, nor how it is achieved, is shown (except that there is a role for Pavlovian conditioning and an artificially inseminated child). In the closing chapter, Susila inducts lucky old Will Farnaby into the yoga of love, but we are told only that this gives him 'luminous bliss', not what they actually get up to. Indeed, he is understandably rather put off when he sees a pair of mantises copulating, after which the female bites off the head of the male. Even when it is blissful, sex doesn't seem to be very much fun, and one rather comes to envy Jeremy Pordage's sessions in *After Many a Summer* with Mae and Doris in their flat in Maida Vale, after vespers in Westminster Cathedral: 'Infinite squalor in a little room, as he liked to call it; abysmally delightful'.

Huxley's relations with women seem to have been interesting and stimulating. His marriages were happy, and he certainly had a long-term and enjoyable affair, without much bitterness or guilt, with Mary Hutchinson. He admired the relationship between D.H. and Frieda Lawrence, among others, and had very many talented and beautiful female friends. His love life, particularly his disastrous liaison with Nancy Cunard, was not perfect. But even given that, his antipathy to sex in his work is very hard to understand.

It is pleasing to record that the one really happy marriage in his work is neither a constructed pose like that of the Rampions in *Point Counter Point*, nor a grim Palanese blissfest. It is that between John and Helen Rivers in *The Genius and the Goddess*. Helen Rivers knew how to die, because she knew how to live. One should be wary of reading too much into fiction, but it has the appearance of a touching and heartfelt tribute to Maria, which she lived long enough to read.

Afterword

It is time to return to the question with which we began this volume; why should we continue to read the works of Aldous Huxley?

Certainly Huxley's world was not our world, and the problems he addressed are not always ours. Global terrorism and asymmetric warfare meant nothing to him; he was concerned with fascism and communism, and danger came from too-efficient states, not failed ones. When he wrote about demography, it was to argue the dangers of overpopulation and the diminishing quality of the gene pool, not to discuss ageing and the coming demographic crisis. Furthermore, many of the methods he favoured – economic planning, conferences of experts – are anathema today. We should expect this – the world moves on. What remains of value in a writer are the lessons we learn from his or her *approach* to the political problems of the day.

I hope it is now clear that there is a great deal to learn and enjoy from Huxley's work. He was an immensely civilised, witty and clever writer. He was not a novelist of the stature of, say, Graham Greene, Evelyn Waugh, D.H. Lawrence, Virginia Woolf or Anthony Powell, and the gap between them and him was compounded by his willingness to compromise his art in the service of clear expression of ideas. But an hour or two in Huxley's company can be a wonderful experience; his essays are often a joy and his art criticism unsurpassed. A turn of phrase can light up a paragraph, even in his most didactic and ponderous pieces.

He was also an important, if minor, historical figure. He was in the vanguard of the 'bright young things' who systematically dismantled the Edwardian worldview in the immediate after-math of the Great War, he played a full role in the 1930s peace movement, and his later thought was an important foundation for the revolutionary social thinking of the late 1960s. It would be hard to claim a deep cultural historical understanding of the twentieth century if one had not read any Huxley.

On top of these, however, there are compelling reasons why the best of Huxley deserves to be read even now, even if one did not wish to read him for pleasure, or for illumination about the mid-twentieth century. First, his descriptions of the nexus between capitalism, democracy, consumerism and technology remain almost peerless. His predictions were not always correct, but he was more often right than wrong – a strong indication of the depth of his understanding of their interconnections.

Second, his work provides an object lesson in how to address modern problems without rejecting the accumulated wisdom of cultural traditions in art and scholarship. Though he was con-temptuous of the politics of his elders and was an important modernist influence, he never lost the ability to learn new lessons from previous generations, whether they be writers such as Shakespeare, artists such as El Greco, or the contemplatives of East and West. Not for Huxley the damaging and arrogant *ab initio* approach to political or social problems.

Third, he diagnosed the important problem of individual responsibility in a mass-oriented and globalised world. His solu-tions to this problem (those spiritual exercises) were not as con-vincing as his statements of it, and he was perhaps over-dismissive of the role of systems, norms and institutions in determining behaviour. Yet many of today's most pressing issues, including our deteriorating environment and the looming pensions, debt and savings crisis, are precisely caused by individual actions, each apparently harmless, cumulatively storing up giant problems for the future. Capitalism and democracy make it very hard to pre-vent such situations arising. Democracy in particular has become a sacred cow, and the hard questions that Huxley asked about it have been wrongly ignored for several decades.

Fourth, one of his key insights was the importance of plural sources of value. No one way of looking at the world should be thought correct; there should be checks and balances. Huxley expatiated on this theme in great depth and detail; very few thinkers in any branch of the arts, humanities or sciences have picked at the multiple levels of significance, description and action as obsessively or as productively as he. Yet today's society, where majoritarian votes threaten to become not only one important source of political legitimacy (which is very desirable), but the only source (which is not), is rapidly unlearning those lessons.

This last theme, indeed, was perhaps the most constant item in a career in which, as Evelyn Waugh noted in 1937, 'like all thinking beings, he is in motion'.[1] Though he changed his approach to almost all of the political and social issues with which he grappled, Huxley remained convinced of the vital importance of acknowledging that (as he put it in 'The Education of an Amphibian') 'every human being is an amphibian – or, to be more accurate, every human being is five or six amphibians rolled into one'. Yet he was convinced of the need for us to understand ourselves, because our amphibiousness 'is a chronic embarrassment, a source of endless errors and delinquencies, of crimes and imbecilities without number'. Much of his work tried to make sense of humanity from all these different points of view, sometimes juxtaposing them incongruously for comedic effect, sometimes trying to integrate them.

Yet Huxley was consciously fashioning a literature for the twentieth century that made sense in an era of science and industry. Unlike many revolutionaries, he was prodigiously well informed about literary tradition. He set himself the task of squaring the circle of creating works that connected simultaneously to the tradition and to our wearisome condition. Whether he failed or succeeded, he understood the dynamics of art, and had keen insight into the intersection between human nature (and greed) and technological progress.

As a result, Huxley is in different ways remote and bang up-to-date. He speaks to an era of science, telecommunications and widespread multicultural influence, where the claims of authority, institutions and traditional values are routinely questioned and found wanting. He can appear, like the poet Greville, cold and unemotional, his work 'all frozen and made rigid with intellect'.[2] He goes in and out of fashion, but his ideas have remained relevant well into the twenty-first century. As the French novelist and poet Michel Houellebecq put it (through the mouth of one of his characters):

> Oh, Huxley was a terrible writer, I admit. His writing is pretentious and clumsy, his characters are bland ciphers, but he had one vital premonition – he understood that evolution of human society had for centuries been linked to scientific progress and would continue to be. He may have lacked style or finesse or psychological insight, but that's insignificant compared to the brilliance of the original concept. Huxley was the first writer to realise that biology would take over from physics as the driving force of society – long before the SF crowd.[3]

Arguably, Huxley's greater contribution was less as a novelist than as a conjuror with ideas whose extraordinary breadth of vision allowed him to place apparently unconnected phenomena into inspired conjunction, and whose brilliant synthetic skill prevented his frequent digressions from distracting from the main point he was making. Indeed, he was often disparaging about his novelistic skill himself, although he was constantly experimenting and trying to find the form that would allow him to make sufficiently wide-ranging statements. He wrote to his cousin E.S.P. Haynes in 1945 that 'I remain sadly aware that I am not a born novelist, but some other kind of man of letters, possessing enough ingenuity to be able to simulate a novelist's behaviour not too unconvincingly.'[4] He wrote of the difficulty of combining ideas with narrative, and was usually prepared to let the narrative suffer to let the ideas come through. The result was often irony first, art second.

Our amphibiousness is often disguised – most types of discourse pretend to a universality that they cannot possibly sustain. This means that our wearisome condition is often a surprise, and creates fertile ground for the satirist. In an essay of 1931, intriguingly entitled 'And Wanton Optics Roll the Melting Eye', Huxley expresses his philosophy of creating irony by looking at the different aspects of the wearisome condition simultaneously:

> Juxtapose two accounts of the same human event, one in terms of pure science, the other in terms of religion, aesthetics, passion, even common sense; their discord will set up the most disquieting reverberations in the mind.

Although 'we live in a world of *non sequiturs*', the artist can, if he or she chooses, make us conscious of all aspects of experience at once: 'So seen, reality looks exceedingly queer. Which is how the ironist and the perplexed questioner desire it to look.' So much of importance is removed from a novel (for example, the effects of small illnesses or bodily functions on our perceptions of reality) that even a supposedly comprehensive account of a world is incomplete. The world of *non sequiturs* would be realistic, truthful, grotesque.

Huxley wanted to know, and understand, everything (in fact, at one point he confessed that he would rather have been Faraday than Shakespeare). Under pressure from his own open-mindedness, Huxley the sceptic morphed into Huxley the mystic. The shift from cynical satirist to religious moralist surprised some and disappointed many, but was not an unknown trajectory for thinking writers in the fraught middle years of the twentieth century, including Evelyn Waugh and Graham Greene. In any case, Huxley was driven by a dislike of the lie, or the untruthful omission. Humanity's wearisome condition is the unifying theme; he celebrated it, and was impatient with anyone who thought life was simple enough to sketch in a theory. He first quoted Greville's 'Chorus Sacerdotum' in a very early short story, 'The Bookshop', published in 1920. It featured over and over again throughout his career, most prominently as the epigraph to *Point Counter Point*, though it is mentioned elsewhere, in *On the Margin* and *The Perennial Philosophy* for instance. 'Born under one law, to another bound': the implications of this he would work out in extraordinary detail. *Point Counter Point* was specifically an exercise in mapping the importance of and difference between points of view; the novel he had just begun at his death (some thirty-five years later) had the same theme.

Thus Aldous Huxley, celebrity, sage, debunker of ideas. The flowers on his tree are many and varied, but its roots go deep.

Further reading

Life

The first major biography, beautifully written and thorough, is Sybille Bedford, *Aldous Huxley: A Biography* (London: Papermac, 1993); Bedford knew the Huxleys for many years.

Nicholas Murray, *Aldous Huxley: An English Intellectual* (London: Little, Brown, 2002), adds detail to Bedford, particularly about the Huxleys' sexual entanglements. It is well written, goes into more detail than Bedford on Huxley's writings, and is now the standard biographical account.

Dana Sawyer, *Aldous Huxley: A Biography* (New York: Crossroad, 2002), is unreliable on Huxley's life in Europe, but is on firmer ground on his spiritual conversion and his Californian celebrity (Sawyer is an academic specialising in Asian religion and philosophy).

Huxley's American years are well chronicled in David King Dunaway, *Huxley in Hollywood* (London: Bloomsbury, 1989).

Laura Archera Huxley, *This Timeless Moment: A Personal View of Aldous Huxley* (London: Chatto & Windus, 1968), is essential as a memoir of Huxley's last years with Laura, but it is also good on Huxley's late philosophy.

Lady Huxley (Julian's wife) left her own memoir: Juliette Huxley, *Leaves of the Tulip Tree* (London: John Murray, 1986). The last chapter is a memoir of Aldous, but perhaps of more interest to the Huxley scholar is the loyal, defiant defence of Lady Ottoline Morrell.

Background

The extraordinary dynasty of T.H. Huxley is catalogued in Ronald W. Clark, *The Huxleys* (London: William Heinemann Ltd, 1968). The focus is on Aldous and Julian, but all branches of the family are covered.

The pessimistic intellectual background against which Huxley's European works were written between the wars is detailed in Richard Overy, *The Morbid Age: Britain between the Wars* (London: Allen Lane, 2009).

The biggest influences on Huxley were two relatively minor figures, Humphry Osmond and Gerald Heard. Osmond awaits a biographer, but Heard has been well served by Alison Falby, *Between the Pigeonholes: Gerald Heard 1889–1971* (Newcastle: Cambridge Scholars Publishing, 2008).

D.H. Lawrence's influence was large but concentrated into a very small period. Consequently, the best account for the Huxley scholar is David Ellis, *D.H. Lawrence vol. 3: Dying Game 1922–1930* (Cambridge: Cambridge University Press, 1998). For the complete life, see John Worthen, *D.H. Lawrence: The Life of an Outsider* (London: Penguin, 2006).

Works

At any one time many of Huxley's works are in print, especially the novels. Few of his writings are obscure, and it is always worth a browse in a second-hand bookshop to see what is available.

The major bibliography is Claire John Eschelbach and Joyce Lee Shober, *Aldous Huxley: A Bibliography 1916–1959* (Berkeley: University of California Press, 1961) with, ironically, a witty Foreword by Huxley whose very existence renders the book out of date. There are many gaps here, and it has been supplemented by David Bradshaw, 'A new bibliography of Aldous Huxley's work and its reception, 1912–1937', *Bulletin of Bibliography*, 51(3), 1994, pp. 237–55.

His essays have been collected in six volumes, edited by Robert S. Baker and James Sexton with short introductions to each volume, although the title *Complete Essays* is a misnomer, and the pieces are organised according to when they first appeared in book form. This has some unfortunate side-effects: for instance, the important essays 'T.H. Huxley as a Literary Man' and 'D.H. Lawrence', both published in the early 1930s, appeared in book form in *The Olive Tree* in 1938, and so appear anachronistically in the volume that covers the late 1930s, rather than the previous one. Furthermore, some but not all of the full-length works of non-fiction are included.

All the volumes are published by Ivan R. Dee in Chicago. *Volume I: 1920–1925* (2000) includes the essays collected in *On the Margin* and *Along the Road*. *Volume II: 1926–1929* (2000) includes the essays collected in *Proper Studies* and *Do What You Will*, as well as the complete text of *Jesting Pilate*. *Volume III: 1930–1935* (2001) includes the essays collected in *Music at Night*, as well as the complete text of *Beyond the Mexique Bay*. *Volume IV: 1936–1938* (2001) includes the essays collected in *The Olive Tree*, as well as the complete text of *Ends and Means*. *Volume V: 1939–1956* (2002) includes the essays collected in *Themes and Variations* and *Adonis and the Alphabet*, as well as the complete texts of *The Doors of Perception* and *Science, Liberty and Peace*. *Volume VI: 1956–1963* (2002) includes the complete texts of *Heaven and Hell* (minus the short Foreword), *Brave New World Revisited* (minus the short Foreword) and *Literature and Science*.

David Bradshaw (ed.), *The Hidden Huxley: Contempt and Compassion for the Masses* (London: Faber and Faber, 1994), is a useful collection of Huxley's essays from 1930–6 on social and political issues, a handful of which do not appear in the *Complete Essays*. These are complemented by illuminating pieces by Bradshaw on Huxley's relationships with H.L. Mencken and H.G. Wells.

Most of Huxley's plays have by now seen the light of day. Perhaps the best of them is *Now More Than Ever*, David Bradshaw and James Sexton (eds.) (Austin: University of Texas Press, 2000).

For Huxley's letters see Grover Smith (ed.), *Letters of Aldous Huxley* (London: Chatto & Windus, 1969), and James Sexton (ed.), *Selected Letters of Aldous Huxley* (Chicago: Ivan R. Dee, 2007), which supplements Smith with over 500 pages of previously unpublished letters.

A wonderful gem has just emerged from the British Library and the BBC. *The Spoken Word: Aldous Huxley*, NSACD72, 2010, is a CD of historic recordings of Huxley from the BBC archives.

Several TV recordings of Huxley from his years of celebrity in America can be found by a judicious search on YouTube.

Criticism

Those interested in specialising in the study of Huxley might consider joining the International Aldous Huxley Society, based at the University of Münster in Germany (http://www.anglistik.uni-muenster.de/huxley/ahs.html), or getting hold of its journal, the *Aldous Huxley Annual*, which was first published in 2001. The *Annual* has been used to publish many of the essays uncollected by Baker and Sexton, and there are even some previously unpublished essays. Some of his plays have also appeared in it, including a musical comedy version of *Brave New World*! Huxley's original writings are supplemented with critical essays.

George Woodcock, *Dawn and the Darkest Hour: A Study of Aldous Huxley* (Montreal: Black Rose Books, 2007), is a reprint of a good account from 1972. Woodcock was an important man of letters, deeply sympathetic to the anarchistic, Kropotkinesque views of Huxley's post-war career.

C.S. Ferns, *Aldous Huxley: Novelist* (London: Athlone Press, 1980), is an attempt to appraise Huxley's novels in his own terms, and those of his readers, thereby giving greater weight to the satires and utopias.

Milton Birnbaum, *Aldous Huxley: A Quest for Values* (first published in 1971; new edition, New Brunswick, NJ: Transaction Publishers, 2006) charts Huxley's journey from post-Great War nihilist to Cold War mystic.

Where to begin

In this book I have divided Huxley's significant career into six stages, each outlined in a chapter. If the reader is interested in sampling Huxley's work in a representative manner, so that each one of these stages is covered, then I would suggest that he or she begin with the following six works:

Huxley as ironist: *Crome Yellow*
Huxley as vitalist: *Point Counter Point*
Huxley as prophet: *Brave New World*
Huxley as pacifist: *Eyeless in Gaza*
Huxley as mystic: *The Perennial Philosophy*
Huxley as techno-utopian: *Island*

Notes

Preface

1 Joyce Cary, 'Morality and the novelist', in A.G. Bishop (ed.), *Joyce Cary: Selected Essays*, London: Michael Joseph, 1976, 154-164, at 155.

1 'Inescapable social destiny', 1894–1920

1 http://www.trin.cam.ac.uk/show.php?dowid=727. This is the only significant mention of Aldous and Julian in a brief autobiographical narrative by Sir Andrew on the occasion of his ninetieth birthday in 2007.
2 From a BBC broadcast in 1964 quoted in Bedford, *Aldous Huxley*, p. 60. Where books, such as Bedford's, feature in the 'Further reading' section below, I shall give only abbreviated references.
3 On the account, for instance, of Murray, *Aldous Huxley*, pp. 140, 179.

2 Ironist, 1920–5

1 Edith Sitwell, *Taken Care Of: An Autobiography* (London: Hutchinson & Co., 1965), p. 89.
2 Murray, *Aldous Huxley*, pp. 69–72, for the evidence of Maria's bisexuality and her relationship with Lady Ottoline.
3 Bedford, *Aldous Huxley*, pp. 132–5.

4 In a discussion of *Antic Hay*, from the *London Magazine*, August 1955, collected as 'Youth at the helm and pleasure at the prow', in Donat Gallagher (ed.), *The Essays, Articles and Reviews of Evelyn Waugh* (London: Methuen, 1983), pp. 470–2.

5 Published in *Vanity Fair* in 1924. Note that this is *not* the essay of the same title that appeared in *Vogue* in 1928, and was later reprinted in *Do What You Will*. The latter, written at the maximal point of Lawrence's influence over Huxley, is even more emphatic in holding up Lawrence as an ideal.

3 Vitalist, 1925–30

1 Reprinted in *The Olive Tree*.

2 Smith, *Letters*, p. 630.

3 David Bradshaw has made a plausible case that Webley was based upon John Hargrave, head of the Kindred of the Kibbo Kift, a strange youth movement that aspired to regenerate the urban population through woodcraft and ceremony, which had attracted the interest of Lawrence and Julian Huxley: see 'Huxley's "Tinpot Mussolini" and the KKK's "White Fox": a new source for Everard Webley and the Brotherhood of British Freemen', *Aldous Huxley Annual*, 2, 2002, pp. 146–59.

4 Sybille Bedford describes the similarities between the real Matthew and the fictional 'Little Phil' in *Aldous Huxley*, p. 207.

5 http://www.dalton.org/philosophy/plan/.

6 The chief source is a piece called 'In a Tunisian Oasis', which first appeared in 1925, and was collected in *The Olive Tree* in 1936. See also *The Perennial Philosophy*, where he castigates Islam's 'black record of holy wars and persecutions'.

7 Smith, *Letters*, p. 266.

8 See for instance Claudia Rosenhan, 'Aldous Huxley and anti-Semitism', *Aldous Huxley Annual*, 3, 2003, pp. 217–37.

4   Prophet, 1930–2

1   Kreuger's career is described in Frank Partnoy, *The Match King: Ivar Kreuger and the Financial Scandal of the Century* (London: Profile, 2009).
2   See the essays collected in Bradshaw, *The Hidden Huxley*.
3   Michel Houellebecq, *Atomised* (London:Vintage, 2000), p. 187.
4   Murray, *Aldous Huxley*, p. 257.
5   *Now More Than Ever*, act III sc.I, 60. See also the discussion in David Bradshaw and James Sexton, 'Introduction', pp. xi–xxvi.

5   Pacifist, 1933–7

1   For Huxley's 'official' view on racial prejudice, see the entry on 'Racialism' in his edited *Encyclopædia of Pacifism*.
2   Alexander Henderson, *Aldous Huxley* (London: Chatto & Windus, 1935).
3   From an important speech given in London in December 1935, quoted in Murray, *Aldous Huxley*, p. 286.
4   This is Murray's opinion (ibid., p. 282).
5   George Orwell, Letter to Sir Richard Rees, 3 March 1949, in *The Collected Essays, Journalism and Letters of George Orwell Volume 4: In Front of Your Nose 1945–1950* (London: Penguin, 1970), p. 539.
6   Quoted in Overy, *The Morbid Age*, p. 252.
7   Ferns, *Aldous Huxley*, pp. 44–7.
8   'What is Happening to Our Population?' in Bradshaw, *The Hidden Huxley*, and *Complete Essays Volume III*.
9   Timothy Snyder, *Bloodlands: Europe between Hitler and Stalin* (New York: Basic Books, 2010), p. 388.
10 Birnbaum, *Aldous Huxley*, p. 97.

6   Mystic, 1937–53

1   Dunaway, *Huxley in Hollywood*, pp. 70–2, says she did, while Murray, *Aldous Huxley*, pp. 333–4, and 335n.31, is sceptical. Dunaway, who

interviewed most of the significant surviving sources, doesn't present a great deal of evidence other than the Huxleys' friendships with prominent lesbians.

2 L.A. Huxley, *This Timeless Moment*, p. 65.

3 C.D. Broad, *The Mind and Its Place in Nature* (London: Kegan Paul, 1925).

4 Aldous Huxley, *The Human Situation* (London: Chatto & Windus, 1978), p. 5.

5 For the history of the use of the term, see Charles B. Schmitt, 'Perennial philosophy: from Agostino Steuco to Leibniz', *Journal of the History of Ideas*, 27(4), 1966, pp. 505–32.

6 See for instance Woodcock, *Dawn and the Darkest Hour*, pp. 199–202, or Birnbaum, *Aldous Huxley*, pp. 153–74, for examples of his sketchy understanding.

7 Richard M. Auty, *Sustaining Development in Mineral Economies: The Resource Curse Thesis* (London: Routledge, 1993).

8 From a letter to Harold Raymond of Chatto & Windus, written in July 1942 (Smith, *Letters*, pp. 480–1).

9 Smith, *Letters*, pp. 718–19.

10 Ibid., p. 516.

11 Ferns, *Aldous Huxley*, p. 209, oddly argues, against the evidence, that '*The Perennial Philosophy* reveals Huxley's commitment to Hinayana Buddhism, whose primary aim is removal from the world'.

7 Techno-utopian, 1953–63

1 His second wife Laura reports him as saying 'you see, I did not realize Maria was dying' (*This Timeless Moment*, p. 257).

2 This letter is not included in Smith's *Letters*. The original French version is printed in Bedford, *Aldous Huxley*, p. 566, and her literal translation, which I have quoted here, in the footnote to that page.

3 Huxley wrote an account of Maria's last days to send to friends; Humphry Osmond made a copy of it, included as a footnote in Smith,

Letters, pp. 734–7. Laura Archera also includes Huxley's account in her memoir *This Timeless Moment*, pp. 20–5.

4 Murray, *Aldous Huxley*, p. 412.

5 Bedford, *Aldous Huxley*, p. 656.

6 Excerpts from which are available on *The Spoken Word: Aldous Huxley*.

7 The Santa Barbara lectures were published posthumously as *The Human Situation* (London: Chatto & Windus, 1978).

8 Laura reproduced three months of Huxley's diary in *This Timeless Moment*, p. 199. It was an incredibly punishing schedule for an unwell man on the transport of fifty years ago. The schedule is also included in Bedford, *Aldous Huxley*, pp. 687–8.

9 Murray, *Aldous Huxley*, p. 444.

10 L.A. Huxley, *This Timeless Moment*, p. 210. The only existing part of the novel, the opening chapter, is reproduced in ibid., pp. 212–38. The remaining text, although unpolished, is well written and makes for a beguiling beginning.

11 Described – and it is a painful description – in L.A. Huxley, *This Timeless Moment*, pp. 276–92. It includes transcripts of tape recordings Laura made of their discussions about the essay.

12 Smith, *Letters*, p. 715n.

13 Vance Packard, *The Hidden Persuaders* (New York: David McKay Co. Inc., 1957).

14 Following in particular Ferns, *Aldous Huxley*, ch. 7.

Afterword

1 In a review of *Ends and Means*, from *Night and Day*, 23 December 1937, collected as 'More barren leaves', in Donat Gallagher (ed.), *The Essays, Articles and Reviews of Evelyn Waugh* (London: Methuen, 1983), pp. 213–14.

2 Ironically, this phrase, originally used by nineteenth-century essayist Charles Lamb to describe Greville, could equally be applied to

Huxley. Charles Lamb, 'Characters of dramatic writers contemporary with Shakespeare', in *Essays of Elia* (Paris: Baudry's European Library edition, 1835), pp. 364–81, at p. 375.

3 Houellebecq, *Atomised*, p. 188. Huxley and his brother Julian appear in *Atomised* as characters, although Houellebecq betrays some ignorance of their biographies.

4 Smith, *Letters*, p. 516.

Index